The Night is Long but Light Comes in the Morning

MEDITATIONS ON RACIAL HEALING

CATHERINE MEEKS

Morehouse Publishing
NEW YORK

Scripture quotations are taken from the Holy Bible, New International Version®, NIV®. Copyright © 1973, 1978, 1984, 2011 by Biblica, Inc.™ Used by permission of Zondervan. All rights reserved worldwide. www.zondervan.com. "NIV" and "New International Version" are trademarks registered in the United States Patent and Trademark Office by Biblica, Inc.™

Morehouse Publishing, 19 East 34th Street, New York, NY 10016

Morehouse Publishing is an imprint of Church Publishing Incorporated.

Cover design by Paul Soupiset

Library of Congress Cataloging-in-Publication Data

Names: Meeks, Catherine, author.
Title: The night is long but light comes in the morning : meditations for
    racial healing / Catherine Meeks.
Description: New York, NY : Morehouse Publishing, [2022] | Includes
    bibliographical references.
Identifiers: LCCN 2022030701 (print) | LCCN 2022030702 (ebook) | ISBN
    9781640655973 (hardcover) | ISBN 9781640655980 (ebook)
Subjects: LCSH: Race relations—Religious
    aspects—Christianity—Meditations. | Reconciliation—Religious
    aspects—Christianity—Meditations. | Healing—Religious
    aspects—Christianity—Meditations. | United States—Race
    relations—Meditations.
Classification: LCC BT734.2 .M39 2022 (print) | LCC BT734.2 (ebook) | DDC
    277.30089—dc23/eng/20220817
LC record available at https://lccn.loc.gov/2022030701
LC ebook record available at https://lccn.loc.gov/2022030702

CONTENTS

ACKNOWLEDGMENTS

Though I sat alone at the computer to write this book, it would not have been possible without the amazing support, encouragement, prayers, listening ears and hearts of so many who have accompanied me. I want to share my gratitude for some of them in these words while clearly stating the inadequacy of words to capture my deep sense of their value in helping me to continue to declare myself as one trying to walk on a daily path of courage as I write and speak about racial healing. Thank you all, and my prayer is that you can hear the deeper message that my words cannot convey when you hear speak of your support and love.

The first persons on every list of gratitude of mine are my two sons, William S. Njie and Mbye B. Njie. I marvel at the men that they have become and their way of being in the world, which gives me hope for the future. I am thankful for my family of origin and my extended family, which is comprised of all of my sisters at the Society of St. Anna the Prophet who hold me in their hearts, cheering me on every day with their love, expressions of appreciation, and daily prayers. It gives me a great sense of strength and courage to know that they are standing in solidarity with me no matter where I am and that they see and accept me with my strengths and weaknesses.

Thank you to my fellow pilgrims who have patiently listened to my laments and efforts to process much of the pain which helped me to find the voice that enabled me to articulate the ideas found in these meditations. They helped me to be able to stay on the path, and they have stood with me without complaint: Barbara Nance, Gail Ford, Tom Brackett, Susan Olson, Roz McMillan, Cookye Rutledge, Bernhard Kempler, Lucile Todd, Jim Hilliard, Ann King, Jennings Davis, and Karen Armstead.

Along with all of these, I want to thank my colleagues in the Diocese of Atlanta, the wider Episcopal Church, especially the Absalom Jones Center, Church Publishing, and all the others who have encountered me as teacher or preacher, read my blogs, listened to my podcasts, participated in any of the other sacred racial healing work that I have had a chance to do. Each and all of you have helped me to keep believing that love is stronger than hate, that courage is better than cowardice, and that truth will have the last word.

FOREWORD

This book by my soul friend and sister Dr. Catherine Meeks was clearly written in the spirit of the late Howard Thurman, Rabbi Abraham Joshua Heschel, and Thich Nacht Hanh who were spiritual advisors and friends of Dr. Martin Luther King Jr. Let me show you what I mean.

More and more you hear the cry of people declaring that now is the time to act! And God knows that action is desperately needed. As Dr. Meeks rightly notes, "The night is long." Indeed, for far too many who have faced years of harassment and the fear of violence, have endured countless slights and the stigma of being *other*—and all of this for no other reason than the color of their skin, the accent when they speak, the persons whom they love—for all these the night might seem endless. Action is needed.

But what kind of action? Action based on rage or revenge simply adds to the darkness already engulfing us. As we have seen too many times in the past, violence begets violence. And action based on selfishness can corrupt the very antidote we seek to end the pandemic of hatred that threatens to overwhelm us. Action of another, more profound variety is needed, action that promotes justice and equity through love. This love—unselfish, unsentimental, unstoppable love—is, in Archbishop Oscar Romero's words, "the force that will overcome the world," and, as Dr. Martin Luther King Jr. asserted, "the only answer to [hu]mankind's problems."

This is action that results from the creative transformation of rage into a righteousness characterized by passion for a better world, a more just social order, a compassionate global community and humanity. We see this kind of action, the Way of Love, in the stories of Jesus found in the gospels. Yes, he was a powerful preacher and storyteller, but he didn't just talk the talk but walked the walk. What he did confirmed what he said! Biblical scholars will tell you that Jesus' actions in the gospels can be summarized into two primary categories: healings and exorcisms. He cured those who were suffering from all manner of disease, and he cast out the demonic forces that were poisoning their souls. He stayed busy, very busy . . . yet throughout the gospels we find verses that reveal the power behind the actions.

"In the morning, while it was still very dark, he got up and went out to a deserted place, and there he prayed" (Mark 1:35). Jesus modeled for us the reality that effective, powerful, Way of Love action is grounded in that "lonely place" with God, as the King James version puts it, and often while it is still dark around us. From such moments, we emerge ready to preach and heal and exorcise the demons all around us.

In these pages, Dr. Catherine Meeks shares profound meditations, deeply rooted in those times alone with God and interwoven with her decades of life experience in addressing racial injustice. The result is both beautiful and powerful, as she calls us to the hard work of self-interrogation, taking seriously Jesus' question, "Do you want to be healed?" If your answer is "Yes," then these meditations are for you, and for all who will dare to join you on this journey toward deep healing and the casting out of the demons that poison our collective soul.

Now is the time to act! And may our actions, our Way of Love and Justice, emerge from the precious time we spend communing with our God, in a lonely place, often while it is still dark. Thank you, Dr. Meeks, for teaching us today in the spirit of Howard Thurman, Abraham Joshua Heschel, Thich Nacht Hahn, and above all, Jesus of Nazareth.

—*The Most Rev. Michael B. Curry*
Presiding Bishop of The Episcopal Church and
author of *Love is the Way: Holding on to Hope in Troubling Times*

PREFACE

The house is on fire, and it's time to stop standing around debating which fire extinguisher is best; it's time to pick one up and begin working to put the blaze out before the house burns to the ground. This book of meditations on racial healing offers one such tool. We have arrived at the place in our shared journey where we are allowing conspiracy theories, distortions of history, fear, and outright lies about race and many other cultural challenges to determine the quality of our lives together. These are damaging and will continue to fuel the fire—until we choose to stop it.

Though issues surrounding race have existed since America's founding and the inability of some to see all of God's children as equal has permeated history all over the world, we seem to have found ourselves in a defining moment in the long journey, and it's up to us how we intend to embrace it. We can stop for a moment and reimagine the way ahead, or we can choose to continue as we have been. When we decide to make true progress, we'll need to reexamine many of our narratives and seek to find deeper clarity within ourselves as participants in shaping the future. This book is meant to help facilitate that work.

These meditations offer a wide range of possibilities for the reader. Some of them will be comforting, and some of them will be unsettling. They will help seekers find many different opportunities to reflect deeply about their own journey. They will challenge readers to interrogate their own perspectives, to listen more carefully to what others are saying, and to be better at discerning their path forward.

These meditations will challenge readers to ask and answer this very essential question: Do you really want to be well?

This foundational question lies at the root of all the work that needs to be done to repair our relationships and our nation. All of us will need to discover how to answer it honestly. When we do that, our answer will help us to know how to go forward—or to know if we really intend to go forward. This book will help you to find your answer and to imagine your way forward as you grapple with our collective future.

Part 1

AN INVITATION TO A
NEW WAY TO SEE

MEDITATION 1

Searching for Inner Truth

Not long ago I was the guest lecturer for a class of seminary students, and I heard myself say, "If you do not do your inner work with sincerity and intention, you will never do anything in the outer world that is worth speaking about." Later I thought more deeply about what I'd said. I've spent the past five decades teaching, thinking, writing, and interrogating myself about the work of racial healing and what I believe it will take to find a sustainable remedy to heal the damage that has been done by racism across the planet. While there are many paths that one can choose, a path to inner work is a good starting place. Everyone has an individual path in terms of the inner work needed, and I've found that it takes a lifetime to do that work.

In the United States and so much of the rest of the world, we have placed far more emphasis on looking outward and trying to fix external sources of conflict. The narratives that we have constructed to govern our lives reinforce the idea that one should not waste time "navel-gazing" or being inner-directed because that is not productive. We are invested in productivity and endless activity as the best paths to follow in the effort to live a fully human life. But nothing could be further from the truth.

The interiority of a human being is projected into the outer world and helps to create that outer world, and until we can see that more clearly and govern ourselves accordingly, we will continue to flounder in unnecessary long nights of suffering and failure. The inner landscape can best be characterized as a community. Personally, I became acquainted with this fact because I encountered many conflicting thoughts about myself and my place in the world—thoughts that were the source of great struggle and suffering as I worked to become a liberated adult.

The inner community is made up of all the narratives that have shaped our understanding of reality, all our personal experiences, and our connection to the collective unconscious. The journeys of our ancestors are brought along with us as we travel the path from birth to death.

The effort that we put forth to avoid inner work by pursuing life solely in the outer domain only separates us from the sources of life and healing that are to be found in our inner communities. As we explore the need, we will call upon Dr. Carl Jung, Dr. Howard Thurman, and many others to help illuminate the nature of the inner landscape and the importance of honoring it. The work requires a willingness to commit to the process of interrogating ourselves. Some may find this idea difficult in the beginning, but asking questions of ourselves and listening carefully for the responses that come from our inner voices is crucial. It is an interrogation because it must be continuous and rigorous. Until and unless we are willing to embrace such a process, we flounder in a state of being managed by energies that we do not understand.

As you read this, perhaps you're wondering, "Why should this conversation be the entry point for a discussion on racial healing?" This is an excellent question. We are failing quite successfully at achieving racial healing in the United States—and all over the world, for that matter. We have invested time, energy, and money and made many kinds of sacrifices to make things better, yet in some respects the racial divisiveness is more profound at this present moment than it was in years past.

In the United States, some things have changed, but so much more must change before we can declare true and sustainable success. We have become more skilled in masking racism, so it often takes a bit longer to discern what is happening before it can be named. Even if we have moved away from having the Ku Klux Klan parading in the center of town, we still see white rage walking the streets in many new guises. Police officers continue to kill black and brown people (most often males) at a high rate, often claiming that they did so because they were afraid for their lives. There was a time when white women declared that black men had violated them in some way, but now we have white women calling the police because they are frightened of black men who are bird watching in a park or simply attending to their own affairs. It is disturbing to see the traction that these claims of fearing black people receive, and the ways in which they are affirmed by the larger society.

We keep asking ourselves how to address these new expressions of racism. We think we can make new rules that will somehow rectify the issues, but that is not the case because the causes are buried deeply in the inner landscape of white people. Deep interrogation of that landscape and excavation of the negative energy found there must be done before healing can be realized.

The head thinks it knows everything, but the heart begs to differ. The heart remembers the traumas, the stories, the joys and sorrows, the lessons of fear, and everything else that has happened to us, and it is waiting to engage with us around all those energetic realities. It is crucial to remember that there are many types of energies operating in our bodies each day. The more time we spend trying to understand them and engage them in meaningful ways, the better our chance of hearing the deep messages that come from the heart—and which can help set us free.

The work of exploring our inner community allows us to become aware of the kind of energies living within us and to be in conversation with them. This can lead to new ways of seeing what we thought we already knew. Such examination of our lives is crucial if we have any interest in being well. We have to engage with the conflicting voices inside our heads and hearts in order to hear the truth about ourselves.

I think about the challenge Jesus offered to the lame brother at the Pool of Bethesda, who complained about not being able to get into the pool when the angel came to bring healing. Jesus' question to him is the most profound one that anybody can be asked: "Do you want to be healed?" In order to move forward, we must resolve the inner conflict of wanting to be healed but hoping to remain the same.

This question, "Do you want to be healed?," rings loudly for all who inhabit the planet, and if we have enough courage to answer yes, then entering into an exploration of our inner community is crucial. There are no shortcuts, exemptions, or ways to pretend to do it. The heart knows whether we are being genuine or not, and it will not find disingenuousness acceptable. This work is mystical in that it is directed by God and draws on all of the spiritual resources that are available to us, but it is not magical. When we embark upon it there will be help sent from many directions because the Creator and all the soul-keeping forces in the universe are invested in each of us making the journey from birth to death as best we can. The ego is the one entity that has a contrary voice.

It wants to maintain whatever image it has formed about the nature of reality and who we are in the world, but that image is the very thing that must be explored. The journey from the head, where the ego reigns, to the heart, with its challenge to that reign, is a long and tedious one that takes exactly one lifetime.

The work begins with a willingness to ask questions of ourselves. Thus we must invite this lifelong self-interrogation process into our consciousness. This process does not need to become immobilizing. It is not about second-guessing every decision we make; rather, it is about finding out what we really think and believe and why we hold those beliefs. It requires us to find out whose voice or voices are directing our path and ask whether they are the ones that we intend to let guide us. We are taught not to ask questions, but each of us must unlearn this pattern as we do our inner community work.

For me, the pain generated when I tried to avoid this process of self-interrogation led me to seek expert assistance. I was fortunate enough to find good counselors and guides who helped me to become clearer about the path I wanted my life to follow and the resources that would help me to achieve this.

This work is not something we can negotiate our way out of, no matter what our outer-directed society says. It does not matter whether we believe that or not. Going through life with our heart closed off from the energetic resources necessary to live fully creates and recreates the world that we now inhabit: one that is broken by psychological violence, addictions, war and other ways of killing one another, racial divisiveness, and too much unmanaged rage, fear, and hopelessness.

Hope for healing in general and racial healing specifically lies in our willingness to say yes to the multiple invitations that we receive throughout our lifetime to search for new ways to see. The first invitation asks us to see life as a journey with points of discovery, rather than merely a set of destinations in which the inner community plays no part. We have to vacate the desire for the security of simply arriving at the next destination. This requires us to be willing to let go of old ideas and embrace new ones as it becomes apparent that they can support our chosen journey toward becoming more aware.

It takes courage to abandon the desire for a security that settles all questions and creates a stable life path that calls for little change. All healing will come to us as we choose to embrace life as a journey with endless possibilities without fear and the need to control. Racism is one of those tools designed to control, and it will become completely untenable when we begin to live intentionally. When we become connected to the energy emanating from our heads and hearts in all the ways the Creator intended, that is when we become fully human and discover where true certainty and security can be found. This is a journey that takes a lifetime.

The Shadow is Calling:
Exploring the Inner Community

Recently an African American friend told me about an incident that will help us to understand "the shadow." He was in a local gym and greeted two white men who were in the locker room getting ready to work out. When he spoke to the first one, he got no reply. He spoke to the second man, who did not reply either. So my friend finished changing and headed out onto the floor, where his workout partner was waiting for him. He commented about his experience in the locker room, saying he thought those white men hadn't spoken to him because they were not comfortable with him, a man of color. His workout partner informed him that both of them were deaf.

This is a profound example of the way in which the shadow helps explain what we do not know by filling in the space between the facts and our feelings. As an African American man, my friend has had many experiences of being made invisible, so it was not difficult for him to interpret his experience in the locker room in the same way.

According to the Jungian psychoanalyst Edward C. Whitmont, the term *shadow* refers to "that part of the personality which has been repressed for the sake of the ego ideal. Since everything unconscious is projected, we encounter the shadow in projection—in our view of 'the other fellow.'" The shadow "represents the personal unconscious. It is like a composite of the personal shells of our complexes and is the doorway to all the deeper transpersonal experiences."[1] This concept of the shadow (and there can be both positive and negative shadow qualities) represents one of the most powerful energies to be found in human beings. It is not acknowledged nearly enough, in part because there is too little teaching about it, and in part because of the great human propensity to explain much of our experience through projections that support major patterns of denial and scapegoating.

If you have read much scripture, you may have come across St. Paul's heartfelt lament: "For what I want to do I do not do, but what I hate I do" (Romans 7:15). Or you may have heard one of the routines by the late-twentieth-century comedian Flip Wilson in which, whenever he is caught in some type of uncomfortable situation, he cries, "The devil made me do it!" And if we go back to Genesis, when Adam is being questioned about his awakening consciousness, he says to the Creator, "This woman that you gave to me is responsible, because she gave me the apple" (Genesis 3:12). Of course, he chose to eat the apple, which led him to realize that he had no clothes on. But the urge to find a scapegoat, someone to take responsibility for behavior that we do not wish to own, is supported by the unconscious notions that we have about ourselves and that our egos help us to maintain. Thus, Adam can maintain his idea of himself as innocent, because he is not responsible; in his mind, it is Eve who is responsible, for having given him the apple, and ultimately it is God who is responsible, because God gave him the woman.

The point is that modern humans do not have a corner on denial, scapegoating, and projection. The tendency to find a way to hold others responsible for unwanted behavior began in the

Garden of Eden. But looking away from that behavior, rather than looking inward and taking responsibility for our thinking, feeling, and acting, is unlikely to save us. The energy to find a new way to see and act must be grounded in intention—when the head and the heart reach agreement that something must change and make a commitment to explore what can be done. As I mentioned earlier, this work is not magical, but it is mystical—and seems illusive because it defies efforts to control it. It requires courage and a willingness to trust that embarking upon the internal inquiry will eventually lead to healing, even though it is difficult to imagine—and especially so in the present moment of disruption and conflict.

So, the challenge before us is clear. The big question is, what can we do about it? While the processes that lead us to commit to the work of awakening to the shadow are complicated and require the willingness to allow for many major shifts to occur in our thinking, there are a few simple first steps. Paying attention to the ways in which we perceive those whom we designate as "other" is an excellent place to begin because it helps us catch glimpses of parts of ourselves that are hard to identify or that we simply choose to ignore. We can ask questions such as: What makes me see them as other in the first place? Are they not human, as I am human? What are the differences that matter, if any? It's important to explore whether these perceived differences are reality-based or simply a reflection of narratives accumulated over the years because they have helped to secure an ego ideal, the desire to maintain a very positive view of oneself regardless of contrary messages that threaten the constructed image. This effort requires the denial of anything negative.

But finding the courage to ask the following questions can help to lead to deeper understanding of one's true inner self: What are the feelings and thoughts created in my inner community around those who are named as "other"? Who lives in my inner community that resembles the perceptions I have of those I consider other? Are those aspects in me considered negative or positive? How will it serve me to change my point of view? How is it serving me to hold on to a previously held point of view after gaining new information or insight?

Another very good way to pay attention to the inner dynamics that are reflected in outer reality is to honor nighttime dreams and whenever possible it is helpful to seek someone with training in dreamwork to assist with this part of the inner work. Dreams can bypass the ego censorship that occurs in waking hours and bring us information from the unconscious that supports the work of awakening to those internal entities that need to be brought to the light. When there are deep and powerful energetic connections to people, situations, and day-to-day experiences that are hard to let go of, there is most likely a message being sent from the unconscious (the realm of the inner community) that is attempting to assist us in moving toward the Creator's intention for us to be freer and more aware of our true selves.

Integrating these unknown shadow qualities into our way of living and seeing them as valued and viable parts of us can become an invigorating source of energy. This inner work will enliven the journey in ways that support our outer work in the world and help to support healing of the planet. It is one of the major remedies for dismantling racism and leading to racial healing. But we resist it because it is harder than going out into the world to fix something or someone else. It requires the self-interrogation and reflection that are not rewarded in the outer world, for their value is not easy to see and certainly not easy to quantify. This is the work of the heart and the inner community, and its success cannot be directly recorded in the outer world. The evidence is presented as we walk on our journey with a new lens with which to view life. The changes will be gradual and easy to miss unless careful attention is being given to the way that our life is unfolding. This slow work of the Creator and all the helping spiritual forces that come to accompany us on this path is always in competition with the propensity to seek the quickest and most economical way to engage life.

For me, I began the journey with C. G. Jung by reading his autobiography, *Memories, Dreams, Reflections.* I started out reading that book as I would any book, but many of the concepts were new to me, and at times I felt like I was engaged in a profound conversation. The deeper I got into the text, the more I realized that I was being accompanied by some type of energy that had not been present before I began. This sense of being accompanied was comforting, though a bit curious to me; it was the first time I had ever had such an experience.

I will never forget the night I completed the book. I was sitting in a prison waiting area while the evening count was completed so that I could be allowed to enter for the class I was teaching. The count was taking a long time, which gave me a chance to finish the book. After I read the last sentence and closed the cover, the accompanying energy left the room. It was a very powerful experience, and although this was more than forty years ago, I will never forget it: it had never happened before, and it has never happened since. This was a very strong statement about the mystery involved in turning one's intention toward seeking a new way to engage life. I did not know it at the time, but I would never again be the same after being introduced to those ideas and possibilities, and it was important to all the creative forces in the universe for me to get the beginning of that process completed in a way that unmistakably bore witness to the value of it for my journey. This was my first concrete encounter with Jung, who was to become a valued teacher and companion on my journey to wellness and my understanding of some of the ways in which racism can be erased from our culture.

Racism's most profound support is grounded in humans' lack of consciousness about the power of the shadow. The external structures that were created to keep racist practices intact are not nearly as significant as the power that lies in the unconscious of all of us. Remaining unaware of these repressed, unknown parts of the inner community allows these external structures to remain intact, with devastating effects for the health and well-being of the planet and all the people on it. Each time humans engage in the intentional work of being more open to the nature of their unconscious and befriending those unwanted and often negative energies in their inner communities, it helps everyone. For instance, when you realize that the manner in which you are thinking about someone has nothing to do with what you really know about the person but is based upon a part of yourself that you dislike, and when you choose to face the truth, it is healing. It destabilizes negative energy of every kind, and that certainly includes racism's energy. Therefore, it is crucial to speak boldly, loudly, and repeatedly about the need to engage the inner community as a part of the journey. This work must be done by all, but especially in communities of faith. It must also be done in the public sphere, where the shadow is allowed to wreak much havoc.

The willingness to accept the shadow as a challenge and to seek counselors, guides, and other resources that can help us navigate this very important part of the healing journey is crucial. It requires courage and the desire to be more conscious about the inner forces that shape the way in which we walk on the path of life.

It can be helpful to find a good spiritual director who can assist you in working through your nighttime dreams, and a good counselor can be valuable as well. In my own journey, I found dream work to be pivotal in the process, and the nightmares that had plagued me for many years disappeared as soon as I sought out a counselor. I concluded that there was a deep inner wisdom seeking to help me to find the path to greater healing by forcing me to pay attention.

It is a good idea to pay attention to the messages that might be appearing in your life that are designed to help you to begin this part of your journey. Those messengers are often quite disruptive until their invitation is heeded.

We Wear Masks

Whitmont's work continues to inform our exploration into the makeup of the inner community and the ways in which it will manifest outwardly in daily life—that is, in our persona. He says, "The term *persona,* taken from the Latin, refers to the ancient actor's mask which was worn in the solemn ritual plays. Jung uses the term to characterize the expressions of the archetypal drive toward an adaptation to external reality and collectivity. Our personas represent the roles we play on the worldly stage; they are the masks we carry throughout this game of living in external reality."[2]

The ego calls upon us to create the psychological clothing that we wear in the world. This begins in childhood, when we find ourselves copying the adults in our lives—for instance, did you play teacher, doctor, preacher, farmer, dentist, or mother because those were some of the adults that were close to you? This early process continues as we pay attention to the cultural narratives, codes, and prescriptions that are taught and that we pick up through observation. We learn how to fit in and to behave in ways that serve us.

As we travel on our life journey, we will be given numerous opportunities to solidify the construction of our persona, which is how we wish to appear in the world. This will be based upon the narratives that shape our lives. The ego will continue to support this process because the stakes are quite high regarding the maintaining of its ideal of itself. There are cultural mandates that contribute to the formation of the persona that will conflict with ideas that emerge from our inner community. Racism is a clear example of this. Herein lies one of the great challenges to white people who have been socialized to create a persona that affirms supremacy in support of the ego's notion that white skin produces superiority. There is so much in the historical record that totally undermines this preposterous notion, and the deeper one goes into that history in the United States, in Africa, in Europe, and in the ancient world, the clearer it becomes that such a notion is indefensible. There is no way to support a mentality in which white skin equals superiority, nor the practices that oppress and denigrate folks without white skin across the planet. That superiority persona has no solid foundation; it's as if it stands in quicksand. As we gain more understanding about the dynamics of denial and shadow projection, we can see quite clearly where the fear and rage that will be addressed in subsequent meditations are rooted.

The most important point that can be made about the persona is that unless there is a conversation between it and the unconscious elements existing in the shadow, it will be a cloak with many holes in it, and it will lead to unnecessary pain and difficulty. The ego is never going to invite the shadow to help it to see better. It thinks that whatever view it holds is quite all right. What will challenge the ego is the deep call of the Creator—or, as Jung refers to it, the Self. The Self is interested only in healing, wholeness, and the well-being of the organism as it seeks to move from unconsciousness to consciousness. For those connected to a faith journey, this energy is known variously as Creator, God, Goddess, Spirit, Ancestors, and all of the other heavenly helpers that we have heard about throughout our lives.

The naming of the energy is not as crucial as the acknowledgment of its existence and one's intention to be open to it and to stay curious and courageous. The God/Self energy requires individuation: the process of learning who we are as an individual, not just as an extension of our ancestors, parents, and other family members. What is revealed in the process of awakening the shadow needs to become a factor in the way the persona is organized and presented to the outside world. For instance, if you discover that you have a lot of inner fears, it is important to address them, because the way the persona tries to mask them and prevent them from emerging is by bullying others.

The tasks of making sure that the awakening process has integrity and that the persona is based upon a truthful representation of the inner community are critical to long-term good health and wellness. For instance, it is important for us not to construct a persona that depicts a kind, generous, loving person without any acknowledgment of our shadow side, which includes some elements opposite to those in the positive public representation. The more of the truth from the shadow that can be included in the persona, that public, conscious face, the better. It means we can feel secure in the way we are perceived in the world without worrying about someone discovering who we really are, because we will be presenting our authentic self.

During my college years, I went to a church where one of the clergymembers was a violent man who abused his family. This person could stand in the pulpit on Sunday morning and offer a variety of wise words and proclamations that helped him to maintain his persona of being a fine, upstanding member of the church community. My sister and I were completely devastated when his wife and two small children showed up at our small one-bedroom apartment one day asking us to shelter them from him, for he would go home after the worship service and abuse his wife, including physically battering her. We were even more horrified and upset to learn that she had sought help from the leadership in the congregation, to no avail; to this day I have no idea whether the leaders didn't believe her because the clergymember had done such a great job of mask construction, or whether they gave in to their cowardice. But his hypocrisy and the leaders' lack of response impacted my view of them, and all their personas were deeply tarnished in my sight from that day forward.

This story illustrates the importance of the persona being a reasonably good representation of the person. When there is such a large discrepancy as there was here, it is a concern for the entire community. The lack of courage demonstrated by the leadership in this church can, unfortunately, be found in many arenas, and it destabilizes people's trust in institutions that need public trust to stay viable. The negative shadow of an institution is determined by the courage that is exhibited (or not) by the people who are involved in maintaining it and to the extent they are willing to be as conscious of their shadows as possible.

It is not helpful for institutions to have lofty mission statements and make great pronouncements about their care as a part of their persona, or public mask, while they act in a completely different manner, one that draws more on the negative aspects of their shadow than on the positive parts. Those statements might be grounded in hope or intentions for the future, but the loudest statement about the group will be what the negative shadow energy dictates, and the truth will be known regardless of their public expression of what appears to be positive energy. It is not simple for the persona to keep shadow energy, whether negative or positive, suppressed. The shadow will find a way to show its face.

Thus, for the sake of the planet, all our institutions (especially the faith-based ones), and every person on the planet, it is a grand idea to try to stride on consciousness-raising paths. Listen to the heart, which knows, and invite the heart's messages to disrupt any energy that wishes to hide the truth. The best and most sustainable work that can be done to integrate the shadow into the persona will require support. It cannot be done alone, though it must be done by each person individually; we all need a community of support, people who will tell us the truth about ourselves. A soul friend, a spiritual director, a therapist, and honest people in one's community will be assets in this part of the journey.

The serious and intentional embrace of this work will do more to remove racism from the culture than we can imagine. Jung declared that if we did this work, we would remove evil from the planet, and while I am not sure about that—I believe that evil is an energy system that cannot be erased so easily—I do believe that evil would be seriously destabilized, because it would engage far fewer heads and hearts. It is the denial and violence set loose in the effort to keep false self-images intact that lead to so much of the negative energy we witness each day. Let's work to imagine a world where the possibility for negative energy to thrive becomes less each day. Every person has the power to contribute to this effort. Try being a half shade braver and say yes to all the invitations to engage in this healing work.

MEDITATION 4

Be Not Afraid

There are hundreds of references in the Bible and other sacred texts about fear, and these texts invite anyone attempting to follow those teachings to not be afraid to do so. Unfortunately, far too often those invitations to live courageously and without fear go unheeded. It seems almost as if fear is sewn into the hems of our clothing—we carry far too much of it with us through our daily sojourn on the planet.

Fear is a weight that we can ill afford to bear. It hinders the formation of nourishing community life. It serves as the foundation for addictions to power, substances, materialism, violence, and many other social ills that we find challenging to manage.

How is that so many of us proclaim that we are people of faith and yet fear is one of the most pervasive energies living among us now? Shootings in houses of faith and in schools produce calls to respond by bringing guns to services and talk of arming teachers, and if we don't arm ourselves, we hire armed guards. Is this our best response to such expressions of fear and the way they have opened the door wide to evil? When massive gun ownership is offered as a remedy to our personal and collective fear, is that the type of community we really wish to have?

The violence in all these instances, where innocent people were murdered, is grounded in fear. The *Oxford English Dictionary* defines *fear* this way: "an unpleasant emotion caused by the belief that someone or something is dangerous, likely to cause pain, or is a threat." One wonders what corner of the universe folks are occupying that makes it possible for them to emerge with the intention of taking the lives of innocent strangers. Some of the murders have been motivated by racism and the hatred that is generated in that energy field; others have been hard to understand no matter how we reflect on them. But we know that fear is deeply grounded in the souls of the folks who act it out by killing people.

So how does working to confront our personal fears by naming them and not projecting them onto others help deter violence? This work opens those fearful places to the healing light that comes from naming the energy of fear and striving to find a remedy instead of choosing denial and accommodation. The most important part of the work is taking responsibility for our own fear. So much of the fear in our country now is clustered around race. In many ways the fear we see now, and the consequent willingness to harm people of color, is a bit surprising, because many of us have tried hard to believe that the country had moved toward a willingness to be accepting of people of color. And even when no one is physically harmed, there is psychological violence inherent in verbal abuse and other acts of aggression.

When we take the time to think about the ways in which othering plays into the fear equation, we begin to see even more clearly why trying to use guns to fix the mess we are in is a meaningless exercise. When someone becomes increasingly afraid of people who do not look like them, allow that fear to override any capacity to be rational, and imagine that the other person or group is a threat to their well-being, a gun does not provide adequate protection.

All thoughtful and caring humans are called to do everything possible to assist in healing the planet, and this includes racial healing. The first step is to make sure that as much energy as possible is dedicated to personal awakening and healing. If we can accept that every act, no matter how small, affects us all, then we can do a better job of proclaiming the value of that work and not allowing it to be minimized simply because it cannot be quantified. Some of the fault for the planet's current situation can be laid on the doorstep of the capitalist mentality, which has taken up far more space than it deserves to have. When humans believe that producing (and especially producing large amounts of money) is the only way to demonstrate personal worth, and then pair that idea with the belief that consumption (and especially consumption of particular types of goods) is a necessity, it is difficult to escape the trap of projecting any failure to adequately do either of these onto people who do not look like us; blaming them gets easier as things get harder for us.

As we think about the inner community inhabitants that we must continue to work to stay in communication with, especially in times when fear becomes more difficult to avoid, it is crucial to pay close attention to ourselves. The disturbing forces in our inner communities, the thoughts and feelings that they give rise to, and the projections that we are making onto others in the outer community can be instructive.

These are a few of the questions that it would be wise to ponder: What is the most frightening voice that I hear coming up in my inner community? Is it speaking truth or not? What do I need to do to ease the fear that I hear from the depths of myself? Is it related to old narratives from others, or is it based in my lived experience? Is there a justifiable basis for my fear, and if so, what can I do about that? What is the name of the fear that is presenting itself? How specific is the fear? What do I know about addressing fear? What else do I need to know in order to keep fear at minimum in my life?

Once fears are named, they can be managed in ways that help to keep them from becoming pervasive and draining off energy. Fears can be addressed, and when they are, some of the ones that have less of a legitimate foundation will stop being part of the conversation. Fears should be acknowledged, but they do not need to be allowed to run around uncontained, because fear breeds fear. Rather, it needs to be met with self-interrogation, then invited to deliver a helpful message of some kind. When that is finished, invite the fear into the light of knowledge, love, and healing energy. Fear does not respond well to dogmatism, so be gentle but firm in the resolve to transform fear into energy that encourages and supports your journey. You will find yourself standing a little taller as you watch fear get farther away.

MEDITATION 5

Let's Talk about Rage

We say no too often when we are confronted by rage. It is not a good idea to refuse to engage with rage. When I moved back to the Southeast as a young adult, rage visited me often and with great force. Often I accepted rage's invitation and there was one instance where I got a sack full of old red bricks and drove out to Fort Valley, Georgia, to express my acceptance. Fort Valley has a lot of isolated farmland. I went to the most remote spot that I could find, got out my sack of bricks and a sturdy hammer, and began to beat on those bricks until I turned them into a pile of small rocks. It was a liberating experience because the truth will set you free, and rage was and is a part of my truth. It was good to find a way to acknowledge that rage that did not hurt me or anyone else.

What is rage, anyway? Rage can be characterized as a space where one is "constantly feeling impatient, irritated, and hostile." It's also been characterized as an intense feeling of passion.[3] Just as is true for all other emotions, rage is an energy that is fueled by many variables. All our experiences, both negative and positive, along with cultural conditioning and cultural narratives, play a part in shaping the inner community. Some of those threads bring injury, grief, and other psychic indentations that lead to a deep sense of rage.

Clearly that rage intends to be acknowledged, and if it is not, it becomes destructive—it becomes a tool for the energy of negativity. It leads those who stay locked in it to fall into deep despair and to seek less-than-positive ways to navigate their way forward. But when rage is channeled into a place where it can become a part of the change-making energy, the outcome is much different.

When rage is acknowledged and managed, either in the individual or in the collective community, it cannot function as a destabilizing, destructive force. But when people do not know what do with rage, it is dangerous indeed. Unfortunately, rage has become confused with passion in people of color, to the extent that African Americans often make great efforts to not demonstrate rage or even anger.

During the turbulent 1960s, there was much concern about "black rage," and two psychiatrists, William Grier and Price Cobbs, even published a widely read book on the subject.[4] White people were amazed to learn that African Americans might be enraged about having experienced enslavement and the subsequent marginalization, violence, and daily acts of oppression designed to keep them in their place of enslavement. In the white mind, all the structures that were designed to keep black people and other people of color in the places of subservience designated for them certainly should not have led to anger because that was just the way life was ordered. The world was constructed based on the power dynamics that favored white people, and it worked best when everyone adhered to that structure. There were many who even thought the Creator had something to do with this system.

White progressives were especially hurt by the expression of rage from African Americans because they were then and continue to be unconscious about the actual dynamics found in the African American struggle for liberation. Dr. Martin Luther King Jr. voiced concern about the impact of white liberal unconsciousness on the civil rights movement in his powerful *Letter from Birmingham Jail.*[5] As he argues in that amazing analysis, the white liberal could naively argue that the liberation process should go slower to accommodate white people's inability to engage in the change that was needed, but this was not helpful. He felt that such an attitude was harder, in general, to navigate than the attitude of an overtly racist, uncooperative white person.

One of the major problems with the gradualist notions of progressives (especially those who are often characterized as liberals) lies in the sense of betrayal that this generates in the oppressed. It is quite disconcerting to believe that someone is standing in solidarity with you in a cause, only to learn later that their position was not what it seemed. In addition, they have the audacity to explain why and how you should accept their position as you continue to live in the throes of oppressive, white supremacist structures. Why should the oppressed have to wait another minute for the oppressor to decide when to set the captive free? The rage that ensued around this and other aspects of white behavior, compounded by feelings of betrayal and deep disappointment, helped to fuel the fires of the 1960s, both figuratively and literally.

The young folks who dared to take to the streets and who began rocking the boat hard enough to toss out a lot of those who contributed to maintaining the status quo were seen as dangerous, and much energy and thought went into developing plans to stem that tide. The historical record reminds us of the savagery that was practiced against groups such as the Black Panthers and Black Muslims and their leaders, such as Fred Hampton, who was shot repeatedly while asleep in his house. No matter how devastating the actions taken against these groups were, those actions were felt to be justified because the groups' rage had to be managed.

But that was then and this is now. At this moment, white rage has burst upon the scene as it did not during the 1960s. Of course, back then young whites were angry about the Vietnam War and other things, and not so much around race. In the twenty-first century, we are navigating a new wave of rage in whites that began before the election of Barack Obama but intensified during his presidency, and of course became even more fueled by the rhetoric and behavior of the folks in the era following Obama. Many whites seem to have felt a major sense of outrage because someone who was black was living in the White House and running the country.

Some elected officials declared on the day of Obama's election their intention not to support anything that he would attempt to do. The mean spirit that began to walk the streets like a stalker continues to thrive today. All of us are being offered an opportunity to pay attention to it and to see what it has to do with us.

This type of energy is begging for a container. It is not helpful for it to be loose in the land, whether in white people or in people of color. It becomes helpful whenever it is harnessed and is focused upon an issue of some sort, when hopefully it will lead the enraged to a place of action instead of immobilization. Unfortunately, too often people respond to this rage by becoming immobilized or by falling into patterns of addictive behavior and deep despair.

We know that rage, left unchecked, will eventually explode, producing dangerous negative splinters. One type of splinter is our massive drug abuse culture. Another is the mental health crisis; we have a serious problem when children not yet sixteen years old kill themselves because they have concluded that this world is too difficult to navigate. A third type was exemplified by the January 6, 2021, riot, when a group of people defamed the US Capitol to make a point about their rage at feeling left out by the powers that be. The very sad truth is that the people who stormed the Capitol are correct about being left out. They are often not considered when political deals are being brokered. In many ways they are put into a position similar to what African Americans and other people of color experience: they are deemed expendable. They became pawns in the power system that they thought they owned. No wonder they are enraged.

This short overview has looked at some of the ways in which our society makes it easier to live in a state of rage. This makes it harder to find places where passionate encounters—as opposed to rage-filled ones—can occur. The air seems to be filled with tension, and that makes it easier for seemingly less serious interactions to escalate into fatal violence. While it is not possible in a short meditation such as this to do an in-depth analysis of all the psychosocial causes of rage and the ways that it can be allowed to become negative, it is clear the intersection of inner rage and outer expressions of rage contributes to creating the culture of violence that has a long historical record in our country. Two of the most recent examples of what can happen when a person's inner rage collides with the rage permeating the culture are road rage and mass shootings.

However, when we begin to address our inner sense of instability and irritation, and distinguish that from day-to-day life in the outer world, it is possible to find ways to turn that energy into a creative force. The work of discovery necessitates being willing to ask a few hard questions: What is the source of the irritation? Is it grounded in an attitude toward others, or in our attitude toward ourself? Does it seem to have a beginning point, or is that an unknown? Is it attached to an event, incident, or personal experience? Is it related to a trauma of some type? Is how it manifests itself harmful in some way? Does that manifestation cause pain to you? Is it useful? Can you imagine life without it?

It may be necessary to seek a counselor or spiritual director to help you navigate this part of the inner journey. This will depend upon the depth of the rage that you are experiencing and how you have engaged it in the past. But it will be very advantageous to the individual and the collective community to do this work and to seek ways to channel the rage into passionate engagement with all parts of your inner self rather than simply allowing it to run wild in the streets of your inner community.

The rage of people who have been deeply wounded by racialized trauma is quite justified and understandable. But that rage still has to be managed, and assistance in navigating it is crucial as well. Unmanaged rage is not helpful for anyone and can do more harm than good for the person who harbors it. All who are rage-filled need to explore how it serves them and how and when it is a disservice.

MEDITATION 6

Can I Get a Witness?

The portions of the journey that have been described in the previous meditations make it clear that if you intend to do this inner work and walk into the large outer world proclaiming yourself as a worthy person, you will need fellow travelers. I like to think of these fellow travelers as the people who would walk over red-hot coals to get to you if you need assistance. They can be depended upon, and their loyalty is not conditional.

Perhaps the most important reason to have a community is to be able to know that there are people on the path with us, and that they are able to bear witness to us by affirming the journey they see us engaging in daily. The lovely passage in Hebrews 11 on the great cloud of witnesses is one of the most profound statements in the New Testament. All those who have traveled on the pilgrim journey are now part of that great cloud of witnesses, the choir of ancestors who are poised to walk alongside us throughout this journey from our heads to our hearts and outside into the world. Those of us in the Christian world hold to the notion that the Creator is present as well, along with a host dispatched to help in guiding us through the life we have been given to live.

The notion of having witnesses to our life's story is a powerful one. These mentors or supporters have walked in our shoes, or are willing to do so, and so they can really know what it is like to live in our skin because they are willing to walk a mile or more in our shoes. Their purpose is not to tell us what to do, though often they can see around corners when it is difficult for us to do so, and they can give guidance, if we are willing to heed it. At the present time, we need more folks who are willing to say yes to the opportunity to be a witness to the journey of another.

I am a person who has chosen to say yes to several such opportunities that have proven far more challenging than they initially appeared. Nonetheless, I knew they would be good for my soul, and they led to a disruption in my journey that allowed me to become conscious. The best example from my life of a journey that cried out for witnesses was my decision to move to Georgia from Los Angeles after college. I had no way to know in advance how the confrontation with the racist structures of Georgia would disrupt my life. And while the Hebrews passage regarding being surrounded by a great cloud of witnesses is wonderful, I quickly came to understand that it was not enough to help manage the challenges of my daily life there. So I set out on a path to find an additional set of witnesses who would offer me another layer of affirming support. My soul found a beautiful collection of them, including Ida B. Wells, Mary McLeod Bethune, Sojourner Truth, Harriet Tubman, Fannie Lou Hamer, and my mother, Malissa A. Jackson Meeks. What a gift it was to realize that my witnesses needed to include folks who were a part of the life that I was living then (and continue to live). Portraits of this group of women line an entire wall in my office at the Absalom Jones Episcopal Center for Racial Healing; they watch me, making it clear to me that I have their love and support but that I also have the huge responsibility of staying on my path with my daily work.

The presence of these women, with everything that they went through, reminds me that I dare not spend much time lamenting my limitations. For instance, my mother graduated from college the same year that I graduated from high school; she had been going to college all my life. Fannie Lou Hamer was nearly killed for trying to register to vote. Sojourner Truth traveled from city to city making speeches but could not read or write. Though Harriet Tubman served as a scout for the Union Army, they would not provide food rations for her as they did for their other soldiers, so she had to find ways to provide for herself. Mary McLeod Bethune started a school with less than three dollars to her name, and Ida B. Wells began stepping up as a sixteen-year-old when her parents died and she took on the task of raising her five siblings.

All these women seem to say, *Remember what we had to overcome, so don't get weary, and be careful about lamenting too much.* It is a great reminder, because there is a lot about racial healing work that can lead one to lament. While I might engage in healthy lamenting from time to time, I always keep in mind my cloud of witnesses. When I find myself turning toward discouragement, I hear them speaking. They know a large amount about being discouraged. Most of Sojourner Truth's thirteen children were sold into slavery. My mother had a child die at birth. Harriet Tubman had seizures that made her everyday life perilous.

Your witnesses can include not just ancestors but folks who are still alive. It is crucial to have folks who can walk alongside you without attempting to edit your choices and disrupt your understanding of what your life is to be about. It is often a challenge to find such companionship; therefore, carefully consider who is being invited on your journey. Many times companions arrive before we have a clear sense of how they might come to be a type of guiding presence in our lives. It's necessary to pay a certain amount of attention to the inner and outer messages that will help you to know who the witnesses need to be.

It is critical for African Americans and other people of color to make a special effort to be witnesses to one another, especially through public affirmations. The trauma of racism has etched narratives of denigration and marginalization into our souls and psyches in a manner that makes it difficult to be willing to do this type of witness-bearing for one another in communities of color. It's important to do it in a more public manner, even if we think that we are doing well with it in our private lives.

While it is easy for anyone to pay more attention to their sense of inadequacy than to their gifts and talents, this tendency is heightened for persons who have been traumatized by negative narratives. In the case of African Americans, we have many such traumatizing narratives to reframe. The process of liberating ourselves from the constraints of living in a society constructed on a white supremacist paradigm requires deep questioning of all narratives, and especially those with negative tones. In addition to this is the daily continuum of navigating racism, which makes the healing work harder because it has not ceased.

Given the reality of the daily life experiences of African Americans and other people of color, it is crucial to have witnesses who continuously bring affirmation and support that can help to reinforce the messages of liberation and healing. The goal is to get to a point where it will be easier to believe the truth about self-worth, and that process will take however long it needs to. The fellow pilgrims who commit to journey with us in this way do not keep score or a timecard. They simply walk on the path and go wherever that path takes them.

Can you get a witness? Who might be your witnesses? What do you need from them? How will you know when you have found the best persons, alive or deceased? Are you willing to be a witness for others? These are a few of the questions that would be helpful to begin to frame with others that will help you in carefully choosing additional witnesses. More than likely, there are folks in every reader's life who are already serving as witnesses. Pay attention to who is walking beside you and see how many of them have brought this gift to you already.

Everyone needs witnesses, and hopefully all readers who do not have identifiable ones yet will begin by reflecting upon the need for such companionship and who might be suited to provide it—and will also find it a great joy to offer that gift to others.

Part 2

NOW THAT I SEE

MEDITATION 7

Loneliness

I knew a person who was more afraid of storms than anyone else I have ever met, and lightning was the worst part of all. At the mere hint of a storm, he would retreat to a portion of the house where he could close all the doors and sit in the hallway until the storm passed by. Afterward, he would emerge from the hallway as if nothing had happened; he looked as though he might have just finished a nap. When it came to storms, he had managed to convince himself that what he could not see would not harm him.

Many among us would like to manage race in this manner. So many times I have been told that a given community has no race problem because no black or other nonwhite people live there. If racism appears not to be a problem because we are confining ourselves to the unlit hallway of unconsciousness, we have nothing prodding us to disturb that illusion. Such a worldview is characterized by an inability to understand the interconnections of all life on the planet and the ways in which all our destinies are tied together. A sense that something must not be of much concern if it can be kept out of sight pervades much of today's thinking, and it underlies attempts to sanitize the narrative of our collective history and make it fit the twenty-first-century projection of our country as a place that is far better than it really is, given the historical record.

None of us is exempt from wishing at one time or another in life to have a better story to tell than the one that is true, but for many there is an inner guidepost assuring us that the truth is going to be the better choice. Thus, the soul death that occurs when one chooses to be unconscious instead of conscious can be avoided by telling the truth. The energy that arises from embarking upon the journey toward consciousness will lead us to spaces of wakefulness where we find new ways of seeing the world, and where we can observe, as if from a distance, how our old ways of seeing and doing encouraged us to stay asleep and unconscious. This can create a deep sense of being beside oneself and wondering what on earth to do next.

In his book *Loneliness,* Clark Moustakas describes such an experience as loneliness. As he puts it, "Loneliness involves a confrontation or an encounter with oneself. By 'confrontation' I mean the direct challenge of facing a conflict, the willingness to experience fear, anger, sorrow, and pain, intensely and deeply, when these feelings are caused by a sense of urgency, loss, or disillusionment. The confrontation shakes up the individual, puts him in a turbulent state and forces him to use new energies and resources to come to terms with his life—to find a way to himself."[6] This confrontation with the truth found deep in the inner self enables us to be resilient as we begin to embrace new ways to see and listen.

The major point to be made here is that in these spaces of lonely confrontation with yourself, you must pose a series of questions that you really want to have answered. The answers cannot be passed on from one generation to the next; if there is going to be any ongoing healing energy generated from the awakening process, each generation and each awakening person must answer directly. And while the confrontation with the truth about ourselves, our families, and our country can result in feelings of loneliness, it is also where the healing energy is generated.

What do I have to leave behind? This is one of the most profound questions that any persons seeking to clarify inner value systems and come to terms with many of the life-and-death issues before them must begin to unravel. Old narratives will not be strong enough to contain new stories; inner work creates the space to see and think in new ways, to produce new narratives. The new work of the soul cannot be put away in a windowless closet; it must be lived out in the light of day.

MEDITATION 8

What Has to Die?

Along the way, each person must ask "Who am I?" and listen carefully for the answer. This is crucial in the work of awakening to all that needs to be healed in both our inner and outer worlds. The answer to this question often leads to a more disturbing and deeper question: "What has to die so that the slow work of the Creator can be done both individually and collectively—for me to do what I was sent to the earth to do?" Your being on earth is not a coincidence; the Creator had a purpose in mind for you, and a part of your task is to discern what that purpose is as you navigate the path from birth to death.

To fully embrace a new way to see requires a willingness to allow old ways of seeing to die. As we move into being more awake, some of the ideas that our families and cultural spaces passed on to us must die. Each of us must find our own way to what has to die, because it is a very individual process that differs from person to person, even though the end result is shared. The result is a deeper sense of freedom because we gain a better understanding of why we behave as we do and where some of our behavior is grounded.

One of the hardest ideas to lay to rest is the idea of certainty or permanence. It is not strange to wish for things to stay the same, because there is a type of security in that notion. The problem with it is that things change all the time. Our bodies are physically changing as our cells die and replenish themselves. Our way of seeing the world may not change at the pace of cell growth, but the call to change is frequently presented. Some believe that we can hold on to the status quo if we try hard enough, expose ourselves only to truths that support our perception of holding on to the present forever, and avoid change. Unfortunately, this idea is simply not supported in the universe, as all things are constantly changing. Being born, dying, and being reborn is a psychological cycle that describes the life journey very well, and any ideas that deny this process need to die.

The inability to acknowledge the truth regarding the lack of permanence undergirds much of the trouble that we are experiencing in our world today. We want our world to make sense to us, and when change comes, we must adjust to the change for the present to keep making sense. When we resist that adjustment instead of welcoming the invitation, the rhythms that lead to healing are disrupted. Thus, having a new transformed way to see becomes impossible if you cannot let go of the old ways. Letting go of an old way to see that was serving as a hindrance can be a great source of new energy.

As we walk along the path of racial healing, we also need to navigate paradox. Parker Palmer's *The Promise of Paradox: A Celebration of Contradictions in the Christian Life* provides an in-depth discussion of this important idea.[7] It is a challenge to learn to hold competing truths in your head and heart, and it is very difficult to inhabit the space created in the area between competing truths. Let me share an example. The civil rights movement was very successful and made this country better. On the other hand, it failed to address systemic racism in the way that was necessary to completely change deeply rooted structures of oppression, which continue to exist. Both of these statements happen to be true. When one can hold this type of understanding in one's head and heart and find the energy to stay in the space created by it, much good can be achieved. But the fundamentalist energy that summons "right" and "wrong" as the only possible ways to characterize competing information cannot be held in this space as well. That way of seeing must die.

Sit for a few moments and reflect: How much time do I spend thinking about certainty and permanence? How much time do I spend thinking about paradox? How do I navigate the space that is created by paradox? These are good questions to explore carefully, because resisting the space created by paradox takes significant amounts of energy. But embracing it can be enlivening.

As the process of letting go of old ways of thinking continues, the questions that you really want to have answered will begin to emerge. These are questions that have been with you for quite some time but have not been allowed to surface. They could not come to the surface until there was some openness created in your inner community to host them. This is not to say that we throw all our values away the moment we receive a drop of new information. Rather, it is a plea to stay curious and open to what is unsettling.

The poet Rainer Maria Rilke reminds us in *Letter to a Young Poet* that we must learn to embrace the unsettling and to love the questions that arise in us. He concluded that learning to love the questions and to live with them without trying to find instant answers is what makes it possible for the answers to emerge.[8] This process requires dying and being reborn many times throughout our lifetime. It requires us to rest in not always knowing the answer to everything. Trust that answers will come if you live the truth that you know and continue to seek to know more of the truth as you travel on the journey of your life.

Courage

Courage is the ability to do something that frightens you. There may be a fair amount of risk involved, and even danger, but saying yes to doing that frightening thing creates a new space where it is possible for courage to grow. It has been said that there is a courage deficit in our country today; indeed, it is easy to see that deficit in the ways we are handling gun violence, environmental justice issues, and racism.

Racism has enjoyed a favored place in too many of our communities, and especially in our faith communities. It has been embraced as if it brought options with it. But it does not have any viable options to offer. Racism is one of the most immobilizing negative energy systems in our country, and in a way it is a thread that runs through many of the other ills that we must engage.

I learned a profound lesson regarding how far the racist is willing to go to resist the truth about racism. For eleven years I wrote a regular editorial column for a moderate-size newspaper in my hometown. While my columns covered many topics, race was prominent among them. I have never gotten such nasty emails as the ones that came in response to my editorials on race. One of them called me a "nappy headed hoe"; some of them implied threats. Though no one made an actual clear-cut threat, the venom was evident.

I was frightened by the level of hostility that was being directed toward me. At the time I lived alone with my two dogs, and I was afraid. I engaged in a conversation with a friend who was chief of police about safety precautions and listened carefully as he outlined my options.

In addition, a group of white men who could not abide the power of my pen went to the publisher of the newspaper to ask them to discontinue my pieces. I will always be grateful for the courageous publisher's refusal to let those men shut down my right to speak freely.

While I was used to not having my ideas always held in the highest esteem by those who thought that oppression was a good idea, I was stunned by this outpouring of anger. I spent a lot of time reflecting upon my writing, as well as the many others before me who had withstood even greater battering and did not allow it to stop them. I thought about what could happen if I continued to write. I thought about the legacy that I had been given by my mother, who always proclaimed that "tomorrow is another day, and you don't know what its blessing will be." She taught me the true meaning of tenacity: "When you get to the end of your rope, you tie a knot in it and hang on." She could not give me courage— no one can give another person courage—but she had given me a foundation to stand upon, and it felt impossible to turn my back on that gift. So I kept writing, because if I had stopped, it would have been a death blow to me, to my sense of self, and to the call for me to stand up in the world and be counted in the face of racism and other injustices.

What I came to realize during the worst part of my column writing experience was that as time passed, I became less afraid. Everything that has been discussed in all the previous meditations in this book requires courage. The ability to act despite being afraid is one of the basics necessary to engage racial healing at any level.

No one is exempted from the work of racial healing. Everyone on the planet has been impacted in some way by race; it is an unavoidable part of our life in America as well as other parts of the world. Engaging with others involves some aspect of navigating race and the ideas entangled with it. And it is not helpful to labor in denial, because that just makes it harder to get to what is causing the problem.

The lack of courage leads to some truly astonishing efforts to create race-neutral narratives. I've found that conversations often move quickly toward characterizing our present moment as "post-racial." This great misunderstanding began to spread following President Obama's election. Clearly, it would take more than one black man being president for eight years to erase racism from our culture. (If only that could be done in such a magical manner!)

Actually, we became more focused on race, rather than less so, during Obama's presidency. We just changed strategy. There were many proclamations from white communities that if we ceased talking about race, we would not have a problem. And while there was less talk about it in many circles, the negativity and anger in whites and the ways they are now being expressed lead to the conclusion that there was a strong racist undercurrent that managed to keep itself well fueled throughout the Obama administration.

As we navigate our way ahead in the present moment, we are reaping some of the consequences of that deepening of silence around race. Persons of any color who had hoped for a real post-racial society saw that hope dashed by reality. And communities of color are trying to overcome some of the new and more subtle ways in which racism encroaches upon them.

We are presently reaping the consequences of our silence around the issue of racism. We can play all the games we want with this issue, call it by whatever name we want, but racism will be here when we finish, and we will still need to engage with it. While it might be frightening to speak that truth, courage asks for nothing less. The following questions can be helpful in the process of investigating the issue of personal courage. How is your courage serving you? What challenges around race and racism are included in your daily life? Do you need courage to navigate racial healing, or have you set it aside while you work on other things? Are you looking for new paths to courage? When you seek courage, where do you go? Do you find courage in that place that stretches you and does not allow for reaffirming places of cowardice?

MEDITATION 10

Faith and Race

Unfortunately, faith and race have forged a partnership that should never have happened. The ways many religious communities have accommodated racism are difficult to understand. While there are many examples from our shared history, two are most vivid for me. First is how the terroristic practice of lynching was embraced in some communities of faith in areas where lynching was most prominent. It is not difficult to find photographs that were taken during a lynching. Many times the lynching took place directly after church services had ended so that churchgoers, including women and children, could have a chance to view it. The Center for Civil and Human Rights owns the profound exhibit "Without Sanctuary," which includes many photographic representations of lynchings and the crowds that attended them, including postcards and notices in local papers about upcoming lynchings.[9] The silence of some religious communities regarding these indefensible acts—and the participation of some religious communities in them—speaks for itself.

Second, after the 1954 *Brown* Supreme Court decision, many white churches in the Southeast led the charge in founding private schools for their children because they did not want them to associate with black children in school. These schools were often known as "segregation academies," as their only reason for being was to avoid integration. This type of complicity with systemic racism is difficult to reconcile with the notion of a Creator who loves everyone equally, but so many faith communities work to prevent their members from seeing this. They do this by telling folks what to think and how to think. One result is an effort to censor history so that it fits a specific narrative, something we are witnessing now in the formation of movements that wish to revise the past historical record. There are whites who want to eliminate words such as *slavery* and *lynching* from our historical narratives. Another result is to create categories and seal them off in ways so that people are left with only one way to think about a particular issue. This happens especially frequently with race. Often when someone in one of these faith communities becomes awakened and begins to ask questions, it does not go well for that person, because their questions will disrupt the status quo if they are allowed to continue with them. For instance, it is problematic when a white person begins to question their group's declaration about the validity of the ways in which people of color are characterized by them leaving no room for their diversity.

I grew up in this racial climate of fear and denial. The lines of separation were clear and always adhered to. So imagine what it was like for me to leave the sharecropping fields of Arkansas and land on the steps of a Los Angeles university, where I had the remarkable experience of meeting white people who believed that race and faith had something to do with each other. Four of these people became my mentors and taught me that white people could see and treat black people as equals whom they loved and respected.

But the bigger surprise was that I came to love them. I had no model for how a young black woman from Arkansas was supposed to respond to the kindness, respect, regard, and appreciation that I encountered in these four white people. They made no effort to force me into their projected images. I was all right exactly as I presented myself: as a young black woman trying to find her way in the world. I learned to accept that they were genuine, and part of that came from the fact that all of them were people of great faith who really believed that there was one Creator. Furthermore, they believed that Creator had made all of us and loved us equally. I had never met anyone like them.

I was learning that I could not be a respecter of persons. The message from sacred texts, including the Holy Bible, was clear: God does not pick and choose some to care about and others not to care about. All are cared about equally. This knowledge is liberating, but it is a rare experience to find people of any race who demonstrate that type of understanding and extend the gift of that way of thinking to you, a human being walking on the pilgrim's path. These four people helped to raise my self-esteem, and in turn helped me to become a bit more courageous about the self-exploration that I had been engaging in for quite some time.

There is no separating race and faith. All the separating that has been done around race by those in faith communities and in other places where denial was more important than truth-telling simply leads to a dead end. Race is forced to become an underground factor in the life of those living in denial, where it can become a negative force rather than one to help move toward healing. Of course, if there is no acknowledgment of the need for healing around race or anything else, then life will be lived without that healing. Healing responds best to invitations.

All the efforts that faith communities make to bypass race simply leave them unprepared to engage with the issues of race that arise in the culture outside of their communities—issues that are going to impact them no matter how much work they put into avoidance. Observe how God is characterized in communities of faith that practice denial of race as a part of their work. Often God becomes a mere extension of their racist thought processes: God is assigned characteristics that support their positions, or they declare that "God is on our side" in situations that clearly are indefensible in front of any right-thinking person, let alone God.

Does this discussion describe your experience with faith and race? Do you see the connecting threads between faith and race? In what ways are you navigating your journey so that the connection between faith and race is a good solid one? Where is the journey taking you?

Faith that has not lost its power should be a factor in helping to create the desire and the courage to explore the issues of race and racism. It should lead to dissatisfaction with anything that does not reveal the truth. It should be uncomfortable with any of God's children finding it difficult to be treated as first-class citizens in their homeland. It should bring in its teachings a conviction and an energy that will make denial very difficult.

MEDITATION 11

*L*oss

There will certainly be losses on the journey to racial healing and wellness. There will be friends who are not sure who you are becoming because you wish to talk about and act upon racial issues when you feel called to do so. Trying to stand up for the cause of racial freedom and justice does not always go well. People lose family members by making such choices. Job opportunities can be impacted by taking such a stand. It is important not to be naive about the consequences of standing up for what is right and honoring one's faith by doing so, especially when it comes to the unpopular subject of race.

One of the places where we are most likely to experience serious losses is within our institutions, faith-based or not. An institution will always opt to stand on the side that best serves its needs. Because of this, consider carefully the price to you of engaging in this battle. Make sure you have what you need in order to engage, and be prepared for the losses, whatever they might be.

During the turbulent 1960s, as we African American students navigated our way through campus racism and its turmoil and got involved with the larger community, we prepared for the possibility of losing our scholarships. Though for some of us that would mean we would have to leave school, we acted anyway. "You can have my scholarship" was a mantra. We had thought about it and knew what was at stake: our scholarships, even our lives. We had considered the cost, and we were ready to pay it.

The main point regarding loss is that it will come. If you stand up for those who need help advocating for themselves in established systems, you will experience loss. Accepting the risk of loss of life, jobs, family members, friends, and opportunities may become a part of your choice to take a stand against oppression. A related caution is not to grumble or blame anyone if you suffer great loss while standing up for what is right. That doesn't make the loss any easier; it just means that you try to be awake about it.

There may be times when you do not have the luxury of preparation and must simply decide to go to whatever is calling you and embrace the consequences as they arise. But as we keep saying yes to invitations to dismantle racism and seek racial healing, it is important to spend ample time thinking about what can be lost and deciding where you stand with those potential losses. This is a part of the process of setting yourself free, so that you can do whatever you need to do. This type of freedom can only come from doing the inner work of exploring potential losses and being clear about where you stand in relation to those potential losses.

As a young professor engaging in campus and community activism, I felt it was important to stay clear about the fact that I could make a living in some other fashion if need be. During those early years, I wasn't too involved in off-campus activism; most of our issues were within the institution, such as trying to get it to step up regarding equity and inclusion. The conversations were often passionate and at times quite angry, but it was clearly the process that had to be engaged in if change was to come. Movement was slow and there were losses, but change did come.

While fighting for change helps to affirm the people engaged in the struggle, there are times when no change can be discerned,

even though there is great struggle and sometimes loss. The work of racial healing has never been characterized as a walk on a flower-strewn path. This work engages with energy systems that wish to stay in power despite the oppression they cause; those systems are not ready to relent simply because it has been pointed out to them that they are oppressive. Oppression is working quite well for oppressive systems. It is those who are oppressed who must keep sounding the alarm, and the longer the struggle, the more it costs.

Have you had a loss related to race and racial healing? What are five potential losses that could come to you from getting into racial healing work or getting more deeply into it?

There will be times when you will wonder why you ever started on this journey. But honest reflection will more than likely lead you to the conclusion that you would make the same decision again if need be. It is these moments, when we have inner affirmation of our way of resisting oppression, that allow us to continue.

MEDITATION 12

Can I Walk This Path?

The only human being who has not asked the question "Can I walk this path?" is one living in deep unconsciousness. The journey of life itself often asks us to query ourselves about walking its path. There is so much to navigate, and there are times when it seems that the things we must navigate far outweigh our human capacity to handle them. But the Creator has promised to always be present, and there is much evidence bearing witness to the fact that our Creator can be trusted. Wherever we find ourselves on the path, faith and grace line that path, along with the gifts that we have to bring.

Life is full of thorny issues, and race is one of the thorniest, because it intersects with so many of the other justice issues that must be addressed. So much has been said about all of this already, so why are we still talking about the path and asking questions about walking on it?

In some ways the path to follow for racial healing work is narrow. It requires a lot of deep self-reflection and willingness to work on what can at times seem to be a lost cause. Decades of work have gone into the enterprise of trying to heal this country of its huge appetite for racial oppression. And while it is an undeniable fact that much good work has been done to deconstruct and destabilize racism, its insidious energy continues to persist.

Racism is much like a chronic illness. It must be diligently managed on a daily basis. There are no days off in the management of a chronic illness: there are medicines to take, exercise regimens to follow, dietary restrictions to observe. As a person who has rheumatoid arthritis, I have learned this well. Living with a chronic illness has taught me much about the way in which racism needs to be managed. It is, in some ways, reasonable to lament how certain aspects of racism continue to present themselves so forcefully when we thought that we were done with them. In our current moment, one of those places is new efforts to suppress the vote in our country. Many of us believed that the Voting Rights Act took care of this issue. Now we see that it did not. But we relaxed because we thought that voting was safe, and while we were not paying attention, much was done to undermine our electoral process. It is disheartening but remains a fact that must be respected.

Choosing to stay as conscious as possible about the work of racial healing makes it necessary to carry this consciousness everywhere daily. When you embark upon the path to explore your inner community and commit to work for racial healing, the work will be life-affirming and life-changing—and it takes exactly one lifetime to get your part done.

There is less chance of becoming burned out if you approach racial healing work from the perspective of contributing to personal healing as well as to collective healing in the community. That way it becomes one of the central issues of your life and is honored in that way. While such work certainly can bring many affirming instances when small victories are achieved and serve as encouragement to vigilantly continue, holding it always as a journey rather than something to be completed is central to surviving.

At the end of the day, doing work in this arena has the capacity to lead you back into your own shadow. It is critical to keep your focus as clear and as nonjudgmental as possible, because there is always the pitfall of projecting onto others when things do not go well. Keep the lines of communication open with people in the outer community, and ask all the hard questions that need to be asked in any given situation where projecting onto others is a risk. Stay ready to reflect deeply upon your motivations.

I don't mean to imply that the work is too complicated to engage in. It is not, but it demands consciousness if it is to be helpful and not just one more burden on those who are burdened enough already. The challenge for anyone engaging in racial healing work is to move along in your own healing process and stay awake to personal issues that impact your perspective and behavior. Racism hides in many places and can create a fair amount of confusion. The only remedy for that is self-awareness and a deep commitment to embracing as much truth as possible around your inner community.

Each of us brings to this work whatever gifts and talents we have, along with our brokenness, and the combination of these equips us to be on this path. In some ways, it is simply the path of trying to live as a conscious and creative human person on the planet. Racism is just one of the places where that consciousness and creativity are needed, and engaging with it can be healing and enlivening.

While each person has to make their own choices about when, how, and where to enter the struggle to heal the land, this is not an issue that calls some and leaves others behind; everyone has to confront this issue in some form or other during a lifetime. Do you agree that doing so with an awakened heart and an understanding of it as a journey instead of a destination seems reasonable?

Part 3

UNWEAVING THE WEB

Facing the Wounds

One of the greatest challenges in trying to find the best paths to racial healing is the difficulty that all of us, black, white, or brown, have in facing the wounds that racism has inflicted upon us. Later meditations will explore some of the particulars of that wounding, but before getting to that step, it is imperative to face the deep psychological truth that one cannot be in either the group being oppressed or the group perpetrating the oppression without being deeply wounded.

In the fifty-year journey that I have lived as a person actively working to teach and lead others onto paths of healing while working for my personal healing, my experience has been that the shortest conversations about racism's wounding are with whites who cannot see that it has anything to do with them. It's an illusion to think that anyone can live in a society like ours, which has stratified along racial lines and systematized the methods of control, without paying a cost.

A fundamental question that each of us must answer is: Who are the victims of racism? And upon careful investigation, it seems quite clear that the answer is "everyone." It is easy to understand why that would be difficult to see for a white person who has been allowed to live in the white superiority bubble, holding on to the notion that the racist constructions are simply the way things are. Historically, that explanation was offered repeatedly as whites tried to quell the dissonance that racism created.

Take a few minutes to reflect upon the level of conflict that must have resulted in the hearts of white children who were raised by black women and who were allowed to play with their black caretakers' children, only to discover that they needed to part ways when they reached puberty. I observed this when my oldest son turned thirteen. Our neighbors, who were white, had a daughter that he played with; the two of them would go back and forth between our homes, and they seemed to have a great time being kids together. I don't know what it was about turning thirteen, but it was then that her parents decided that she could no longer come to our house; following their decision, we kept him from going to their house. Of course, one of the greatest fears in the mind of unconscious white parents is that their child will form alliances with blacks that will evolve into sexual liaisons instead of helping to maintain the racist constructions designed to control and maintain this indefensible system. The historical record is quite clear about that fear and the many acts of violence that have been perpetrated in an effort to manage it; lynchings were only the most egregious. The irony is that white men, especially during slavery, have seemed to find the formation of sexual liaisons with black women quite acceptable, as Lillian Smith reminds us in her insightful *Killers of the Dream*.[10] But these liaisons were confusing for everyone and contributed to much racialized trauma, as will be addressed in a later meditation.

The conflict between words and actions exhibited by many white men created confusion in the hearts of those who heard what was being taught while observing behavior that sent an entirely different message. Along with this were the positive messages that were given to white children by the black women who cared for them and loved them despite the circumstances of their work environment and their personal lives. For the past fifty years, I have listened to so many stories in racial healing workshops about the profound relationships that whites had with blacks, mostly women, who worked for their families during their childhood and at times in their adult lives. While these stories often revealed troubling levels of unconsciousness about the lives of the folks being remembered, they are a part of the narratives that helped to form the storytellers' lives, and they must be respected as such.

Those connections were fraught with blindness that prevented whites from being able to clearly see black women and men as equal humans. Though the connections were real and made deep impressions upon those living amid the dissonance created by the double messaging, it was necessary to create a way to manage that confusion, and the remedy was to create categories of blacks. One of the most devastating categories arising out of that process is the "exceptional negro." That category was (and to some extent continues to be) reserved for the black person who is favored by whites for filling a set of satisfactory roles. In days gone by, the people in that category were usually blacks who were servants; now they tend to be blacks who behave in ways that present no sense of threat to whites or who have achieved much and whose inspiring stories confirm whites' projection of who they should be. It is a very unhealthy space to occupy, and it is costly to maintain.

There are extremely large amounts of baggage to be explored in all communities of color and the white community around the issue of interracial love and marriage. Even today, prohibitions against such connections still exist in some legal codes. Though some of the stigma has subsided, there continues to be a surprising amount of emotion involved with such relationships, and in particular regarding connections between white women and black men. I recall the gravity of that issue in the 1970s and 1980s, especially in professional communities, when black women expressed much rage regarding those connections.

If you are a reader of color, what has been your experience with this issue of being seen as an exception? If you are a white reader, how has this part of the journey with race been for you? What, if any, early relationships did you have with blacks and other people of color that became an important part of your narrative?

The wounds caused by racism are not simple to manage, and it is impossible to do so if they are allowed to go unacknowledged. The longer these wounds remain unaddressed, the more disruptive they can be.

MEDITATION 14

Racialized Trauma

Racialized trauma is the net effect on people of color after experiencing a stressful racist incident, and can be identified by physical and psychological symptoms that follow such an incident. Some of the psychological symptoms include fear, aggression, depression, anxiety, low self-image, shame, hypervigilance, pessimism, nightmares, difficulty concentrating, substance abuse, and relational dysfunction. Physical symptoms may include hyperactivity, heart disease, and headaches.[11]

Presently there is a fair amount of debate about whether racialized trauma can be passed from one generation to another. The field of epigenetics studies the ways in which the transmission of information from one generation affects the next generation. While some studies are inconclusive about whether racial trauma can be passed down, other research indicates that while the mind might forget, the body does not—that deep in every cell is a trace of memory of every event we have experienced and the sensations and feelings that occurred with them.[12]

My understanding of this leads me to believe that it is important to be careful about the way traumatic events are processed. We must not be too hasty to label racist incidents as microaggressions and try to minimize them, since the experience of the trauma will not be forgotten.

I recall an incident that highlights this point quite well. When my oldest son was in middle school, he traveled to a south Georgia town with his Quiz Bowl team for an overnight trip. As he and his team were walking from a nearby restaurant back to their hotel, they were accosted by a local law enforcement officer. The police officer seemed to be having a bad day, since he chose to harass a child. He pulled his car up beside my son, rolled down his window, and asked my son, "Do you want some peanuts?" My son said, "No, sir." Then the officer said, "Well, you should, because you look like a monkey." This remark frightened my son, who was not expecting to be terrorized by a police officer. He was thirteen years old.

When he returned from the trip, he told me about it. I don't recall ever being as enraged, before or since. The idea of a person who is supposed to be a grown-up choosing to harass a child when he should have been trying to make sure that child was safe was almost too much to take. It took major willpower on my part not to get in my car with my son and drive down to that town to allow this bully to apologize, but there was no way that I could do that at the time. Because the next best thing for a writer is to write, I wrote the sheriff in that jurisdiction to report the incident. I must say that the sheriff was himself appalled by the incident and very apologetic. I told him that the officer needed to apologize to my son.

My son had told me not to bother reaching out to them because they would not do anything about it. I begged to differ with him. About a week later, he received a long letter of apology and a replica of a badge as part of the apology. When I handed the letter to my son, he looked at me in disbelief. After he read it, he had the biggest grin that I had ever seen on his small face. He said, "Mama, he actually wrote me, and he apologized. I am so surprised." Even at the tender age of thirteen, he had taken in the message that he simply had to live with aggressions against him as a black person. It was my job to help interrupt that negative narrative to the best of my ability.

While it is impossible to protect yourself or those you love from racist acts such as this, the ways in which they are responded to can create an alternative narrative or at least a narrative to run alongside it. That new narrative can bring enough energy to mitigate the damage done to the psyche by the initial incident. First, one needs to know that this type of behavior does not have to be tolerated; when the racist incident occurs, it is important to speak about it then and there instead of trying to swallow it or reshape it in some manner. And when it comes to children, it is critical for them to understand that they are not up against that kind of dehumanizing bully by themselves. My sons never had to wonder about that.

So when the memory of that incident comes up out of my son's inner community, he can bring up the additional narrative about something being done about it. He did not simply become a victim. He was a victim, yes, but he was shown that he had a recourse. Little did I know he would get to have this experience more than once. The next incident was with one of his teachers who made fun of his name and the name of his best friend. My son is a native of Gambia, in West Africa, and his best friend is from Nigeria. The teacher thought that their names were contrived by African American parents who were trying to give their children odd names. She did not know that these two children were African, not African American, so she mocked their names in front of other children. Of course, their friends told them what she said. When he told me, I decided to go speak to her about her disrespectful behavior. She was quite contrite and made lofty promises about apologizing to them when she saw them in class. I told her that she needed to send them written apologies. She did.

These examples are being shared as some of the ways that adults (and parents in particular) need to make sure to stand up for children against these types of microaggression, so the children know that they are not alone in a world that wants to bully them and denigrate them. They also need to see adults being held accountable for bad behavior and having to show respect to them. Just as the body's cells can remember the negative vibrations, they will hold the positive memories also. I believe that there is the possibility of interactions between the two types of cellular information as children travel on their paths and that it will make a difference in the quality of their life journeys.

Though much has been said about helping our children deal with racist incidents, it is important for adults to attend to themselves in a similar fashion. It is crucial to hold the perpetrators of such behaviors accountable in all possible ways. This leads back to our earlier meditations on the inner community. If the inner community receives the message that it is possible to resist abuse, it will have a better chance of defending itself against trauma to the psyche. People of color must work to learn better ways to navigate racial trauma because it will be here as long as racism exists, and it does not appear that we will be rid of it for many millennia to come.

Furthermore, the perpetrators of racist comments and behaviors are traumatizing themselves without realizing it. It is not possible to behave in such ways without it affecting their psyche. Perhaps the energy behaves differently than it does in those who suffer such denigration; nevertheless, wounding occurs. It is important for whites to understand that all the racist incidents that they participate in or enjoy will leave scars on their psyche and in their soul, impacting their lives; the cells do not forget. We need to talk much more in our efforts to heal racism about the wounding that whites experience, and much work needs to go into naming what is seen. Predominantly white communities are quite sure that they have escaped racism's wounds and that all they need to do is turn to new ways of seeing when possible and try not to cause harm to any person of color. But that is not good enough, because it is too easy to become complicit with the racist structures that make up the status quo and to get pulled into the undercurrent of it, often unconsciously.

If you are a person of color reading this book, spend a bit of time walking back through the doors of your life to see if you find racialized trauma. Where is it lurking? How does it destabilize you? How do you engage it, if you do? If you are a white person reading this book, do you find it difficult to see yourself as being wounded by racism? If not, why not, and if yes, how? Do you have any ideas about how to navigate through racialized trauma with people who are not white? Can you imagine how racism has wounded you and others you care for who happen to be white?

Racism's insidiousness allows it to reorganize itself quickly and often. It is easy to be seduced into thinking that all is well when there is a grave need for deep reflection. The healing light longs to bring its power into predominantly white communities, to help them wake up from the long sleep of denial and the strange belief that one can live in a racist society, benefit from racism, be racist oneself, and somehow escape the negativity that comes from choosing that path instead of the path to awakening.

MEDITATION 15

Look in the Right Place

There is a lovely Sufi story about Mulla Nasrudin, who lost his key. He was outside looking for it, down on his hands and knees. One of his friends came upon him while he was searching and asked him what he was doing. "I lost my key," Mulla Nasrudin told him. So his friend began to help him search, to no avail. Finally the friend asked him, "Where did you lose the key?" Mulla Nasrudin replied, "I lost it in the house, but the light is better out here."[13]

Yes, the light is better out here, but the dark places are where many of the answers lie. In order to find the path we need to travel to get to the truth for ourselves; we must be willing to seek the truth in the places where we are likely to find it rather than in the places that suit us. Of course, there can be a few rare times when the answers are where we expected to find them, but most of the time we will be surprised by the places where the answers are hidden.

The search for inner personal truth demands attention. It is important to make sure that what you are seeking is actually the truth and not validation for a set of behaviors that need to be left behind. For instance, if you invite people in your church or social community to help in the search, make sure to choose people who are likely to be honest and won't simply verify the status quo. This search for the truth will not be pleasing to the ego, which is invested in holding on to things as they are, and it will find as many ways as possible to subvert the process.

One of the ways that this process can be derailed is by looking for quick fixes that might work for others but are far from being the correct path for you. There is no one-size-fits-all pattern that can be followed as you seek to discover the way forward to racial healing, both for yourself and for others. Rather, pay attention to where your energy leads you.

Generally, the urge that prompts you to take action is accompanied by pain. While it would be nice to begin the search simply because it's a good way to behave, that's rare; there is usually a painful or at least disturbing catalyst involved in the process. If those early urgings are not honored, they become more and more painful until they are acknowledged.

Racism lies and pretends that some things do not matter or have nothing to do with race. One of the most common forms of this lie involves microaggressions. It is easy for the ego to talk either the victim or the victimizer out of seeing those microaggressions for what they really are. When this is allowed to happen, the behavior persists. For example, an African American woman shared with me that she had been insulted by a white person, but she quickly added that it did not matter. However, it was clear to me how much this incident had hurt her.

The ego is very good at covering up what it does not wish to acknowledge. When we catch a glimpse of an inconvenient truth, the ego facilitates turning away from it by projecting it onto someone or something else. The refusal to name things for what they are makes it hard to know where to look for them. While naming does not always result in change, when things are not named they will rarely change. There is great power in being able to call internal and external experiences by their proper names.

This exploration requires us to listen carefully. Opportunities to listen surround us but cannot be entertained until the noise inside our heads and hearts is quieted. The process for achieving that quieting involves practicing silence, as the ancient monk Brother Lawrence speaks about in his book *The Practice of the Presence of God*.[14] There are many paths to the silence that allows us to focus. One path involves ceasing to use busy-ness as a buffer against silence. When confronted with silence, what do you do? Do you welcome it? Do you invite it to sit with you even if it brings pain? When we stop the frantic pace that characterizes so much of modern-day life, the moments of stillness and quietness that ensue can lead us to see more of what is to be seen and heard, supporting our healing process.

The confrontation with loneliness that was reflected on in an earlier meditation should not be overlooked as another way to practice silence. The same is true of the encounters with grief that can bring the noisy inner community to silence when we allow it. In the space that is created by these confrontations, we can often begin to discern what needs to be allowed to come to the surface for reflection. Be aware, though, that one of the most profound attributes of grief is that when it knocks on the door of our hearts, it brings its entire family with it. When we open that door, as we should, it is important to be prepared to encounter multiple memories of grief.

This was illustrated quite profoundly as I recovered from having two hip joint replacement surgeries within three months. For the first surgery, I paid a bit of lip service to the idea of saying goodbye to the hip joint that was being replaced by the implant, and my recovery was speedy. Clearly, though, I did not finish the work that needed to be done, because during the recovery from the second surgery, I had a powerful visitation of grief regarding the loss of two hip joints, along with layers of grief from other periods of my life. I felt a great temptation to busy myself in various ways to skip some of the immobilizing energy that accompanies grieving, but I did not. Instead, I spent several days allowing the grief to simply be present and immobilizing. It was not depression but deep grief about the loss of a part of my body and my image of an earlier view of myself, but it awakened memories of old, unresolved losses. The depths of the grief were a bit disconcerting, but staying with it and moving through it resulted in a new sense of energy and willingness to courageously move forward through whatever new grief may come to me.

Inner liberation allows us to become free to engage in racial healing without having to make projections to avoid the pain of racism or attempting to hold others responsible for the damage it causes. The free person simply acknowledges what can be done and what cannot be done, then moves forward on their path with humility and courage.

MEDITATION 16

The Search for Remedies

I lived a lot of my early life being certain that Mama was going to poison us with one of her home remedies. She had a remedy for everything. I regret now that I did not pay more attention to her treasure trove of remedies, though I have come to discover a few on my own. But despite that childhood concern, I respect her genius and know that it is important to pay attention to the natural healing properties of herbs, essential oils, and other gifts that can be found growing in our woods and yards.

When it comes to remedies for racism and all its ways of wounding, however, there are no shortcuts, and what is a solution for one person may not have positive effects for another. I get so many inquiries at the Absalom Jones Episcopal Center for Racial Healing from people seeking a prescriptive fix for some aspect of racism, and there are days when I wish that I could give them what they're seeking. But on my better days, I know that wouldn't serve them well. The remedy for internal injuries caused by racism must come from engaging racism at its core, as this entire book of meditations argues. The work is mystical, not magical. I have said that before and will say it again, because it is difficult to believe. But the search for a prescription is basically the search for a magical answer.

"What can I do?" This is the question that is asked by so many whites as they become more conscious of their racist wounding. The question implies that there is a formula, a prescription that can be found somewhere, and that the work is to find the person who knows what it is and have them share it. This is a very dangerous response to awakening consciousness because each person has to find their own way and the personal energy needed to engage their search. In fact, the work of the person asking that question is to find the answers that lie inside them. The most important thing to do is stand still, listen, and, as the poet David Whyte reminds us, "don't take the second step / or the third, / start with the first / thing / close in, / the step / you don't want to take."[15] The way to discover this is to listen to your heart and to carefully assess whether you have truly discerned the work that belongs to you. It is a major mistake to embark upon tasks to dismantle racism in the outer world simply because it is a good idea for someone to do it. Many questions need to be asked and answered before you undertake such tasks, because when it is not what you are called to do, it will be very difficult if not impossible to sustain the effort. There are numerous examples of good initiatives that died an early death because folks were attempting to do the work in ways that didn't provide the energy needed to sustain them. We call it "burnout," and it may be that folks do feel burned when they must face that type of failure. But it could have been avoided by standing still a bit longer and realizing that perhaps a shorter-term initiative would have been better, or a completely different path should have been taken in the first place.

While the person waking up can be wounded by acting in haste, it is also possible to cause harm in communities where there is great need and whites show up promising to offer a particular service but disappear too quickly. In such cases it would have been better for all concerned to go slower and clarify the next steps. Awakening consciousness is very exciting and energizing, but it must first become grounded in a new way of seeing. Connecting that new way of seeing with the head and heart is crucial and important work. It is the responsible way to handle new understanding, and it creates the possibility for an even greater understanding to emerge over time.

White people tend to gravitate toward communities of color when they begin to wake up to racism, but it would be more helpful in many ways for them to look toward other whites first as they seek to find ways to share their newfound liberation. Of course, doing that is much harder than simply appearing in a black or brown community as an anonymous rescuer. To speak to those you know about your new understanding of the indefensibleness of the systems of oppression that have been constructed in our country is challenging. But after you have stood still and listened, remember what the poet has instructed: do the first thing first.

What is that first thing? How does the newly awakened person avoid becoming immobilized by the fear of offending another or simply appearing foolish? There will be times when the newly awakened person will appear foolish and times when they do or say something that causes offense. When that happens, the person will apologize and move on. When someone points out a fault with some part of what is being said or done, it is important to listen and sit with it until it comes into focus enough to be engaged. The point of trying to offer a healing remedy is to make sure that it turns out to be truly a source of healing.

As I write about seeking remedies, I realize that one could simply say that the process is too complicated, so it might be better to stay home and do nothing. I do not believe that doing nothing in the face of injustice and behaviors that hurt others should ever be a choice, but it is true that one should stay home until there is a clear-headed sense of the best way to offer help in communities of color. Many communities of color across the United States have suffered from too many false starts and broken promises. One of the major examples of such action was the Weed and Seed program, which was designed to rid designated communities of crime and replace it with positive behaviors, by the Clinton administration during the misguided "war on drugs" era. There was far more talk about doing good during that time than the good that was actually achieved.

During part of this era, I served as a loaned executive to the mayor of Macon, Georgia, and I was able to clearly see the shortcomings of this initiative, especially regarding its promises to revitalize so-called blighted neighborhoods. While there were numerous erroneous assumptions made by those who crafted the Weed and Seed initiative, perhaps the most egregious one was the assumption that the targeted communities—which in our case were black—had no resources of their own. Of course, many of the people were poor, but there are always resources to be found in a community, though they may draw more on people's spiritual and psychological capital than on their financial means. It is a tragedy when those resources are denigrated; when an outsider decides that the people of a community have no resources, that act disempowers them in ways that make it impossible for them to imagine themselves as having any agency. Furthermore, there is a profound sense of arrogance involved in assuming that anyone knows best for another person who is not a child living in their house.

Perhaps the next most important thing to do after listening carefully and paying close attention to the feedback that comes when any kind of critique is being given is to ask, "How can I be helpful?" or "What do you want?" People of color and others struggling with oppressive systems have the capacity to know what they want and need, and they will speak about those needs and desires if given a chance. So, asking the folks that you have chosen to help how you might be helpful is a good rubric to follow before rushing off to make change for them based upon your assumption of their need. This is so whether you are one individual or a government agency or anyone else who has the power to help. The ability to offer help to another lies first in having the respect to take the time to find out what is needed—or, better still, what is the desire of their heart. The arrogance of outsiders who wish to serve thinking that those who are to be served can't possibly know how to speak about their needs is prevalent in many of the communities that do need help.

There is a very strange sight in the middle of Juffure, the Gambian village that is the ancestral home of *Roots* author Alex Haley: a streetlight. It is my understanding that an overzealous visitor to the region thought that this tiny village, which is very dark at night, as is most of the country, needed a streetlight. So they bought one and took it there. The major problem, which the visitor either had forgotten about or did not know, was that there was no electricity in that part of the country, so the light sat there night after night, unlit for almost two decades. This is a giant monument to what happens when we make assumptions. The truth is that the local people were quite all right with the darkness at night because they had come to appreciate the beauty of the night sky; but more than likely there were other things that could have been brought to their village that would have been helpful to them and appreciated.

Clearly, the arrogance of making choices to carry out certain good projects in a community without involving anyone in that community should be avoided. Deep reflection will highlight the necessity of reserving the offer of service for those with whom there is a sense of connection and a fair amount of communication. The willingness to engage in this way is grounded in developing profound respect for the people one is seeking to serve.

This very passionate discussion of protocols for those wishing to assist communities of color must be paired with the notion that members of such communities have to speak a bit louder about their needs. They need to work very hard to find or reclaim as much of their voice as possible, so that they will not devolve into behaving as if anything at all will do for them. They are not compelled to be grateful for things that do not serve them, even if they need assistance.

Those who wish to assist communities of color can consider taking the time to engage in conversations with community members long enough to model what agency looks like. Their willingness to show that type of respect and care might become the best gift they can give.

MEDITATION 17

It is Not Magic

Much effort has been expended across the years trying to find a magic cure for racism. The one that has been used the most and has failed repeatedly is the call for beloved community. When Dr. King spoke about beloved community, he was imagining the creation of spaces where the structures of oppression had been banished and replaced by a spirit of understanding in which every person is acknowledged to be God's beloved child. In such spaces, everyone has the right to explore how to become the person that God sent them to the earth to be. These spaces would offer a new way to see and to be in a world that did not have the intention to allow black and brown people to inhabit it. Dr. King spoke powerfully about the inextricable connections between whites and people of color in the journey to true and sustainable liberation. Beloved community was not ever just about pulpit swaps and potlucks, as we have allowed it to devolve into.[16] The ways in which the idea is spoken about present a challenge, because beloved community is not something that can be manufactured by humans; instead, it is a gift that is given in mysterious ways as humans work to remove the barriers to caring about one another.

We must approach the idea of beloved community as a process of making space in the head and the heart so that God can enter that space with energy that creates something new. There is so much talk about this idea these days that we must wonder if we are clear in what we are seeking. Are we seeking a place where systemic oppression does not rule? Are we seeking a place where all are welcome and loved? Are we seeking a place where racism will be so unwelcome that its energy would die? Do we really want everyone to have what they need? Do we have any interest as a people in trying to find the paths that will help us to vacate our self-centered attitudes and envy? Do we really have the desire to have communities of equality where folks are more focused upon what is good for the whole than on getting more for themselves?

Beloved community is born when there is a genuine willingness to listen to one's heart, try to discern its call, and commit to trying to find a path that will allow us to respond to whatever it asks of us. Our openheartedness births something that was not present before we engaged in that process: an empowered way to be together. It is in these spaces that radically new ways to see and behave emerge; it's not just a matter of adding a new layer of paint to old ways. Beloved community is truly a gift from God.

Understanding that beloved community cannot be manufactured gives us a better chance of appreciating it as something mystical, a gift from God, something that is not controlled by earthly behaviors. That understanding sets us free to open our hearts to the message that there are no second-class citizens in God's world. There is one Creator in the universe who has created everyone and not many creators who have made categories of humans with diverse values. This is an issue that is very necessary to become clear about as we seek to see everyone as children of God who are loved equally.

Why Black People Are Still Talking about Race

Racism's energetic power makes it necessary to make sure that the conversations about it do not cease until it is dismantled. If the structures that undergird racism were not in such good shape, perhaps the conversation could cease. While in the past decades some oppressive structures have been destabilized, too many of them continue to be alive and well. Thus all people of color, and especially African Americans, are compelled to continue to talk about race.

Whites who lament their weariness about the conversation on race simply have no idea what it is like to be a person of color who must live each day with the weight of racism's burdens. As one of my sons told me some years ago, "Mama, it is so hard to be black in America." This sentence broke my heart, not because I did not know that already, nor because I did not feel the weight of living as a black person here, but because he was so young yet already knew it. My dream for my sons was for them not to have to experience the difficulty of being black in this country.

Oftentimes, when whites hear us talk about what it is like to navigate each day in a black body, they find it troubling, and I have heard many say they wish that the conversation would cease or that they simply want to remove themselves from it. The fact that there is an option for whites to remove themselves from the conversation is one large example of what it means to have privilege: the privilege to enter this struggle when and where it is convenient. It is indeed an enviable place to live. But where do black people and other people of color go to take a break from the conversation? Nowhere, because there is no place to go; you take yourself with you wherever you go, and the gift and burden of being black is always present. So, until we create a world that is not stratified on the basis of skin color, the conversation is here to stay.

As a matter of fact, part of the remedy for being able to stay on the path as a black person—or as a person of any other skin color—is the ability to talk about the experiences of racism. It is a very healthy act to name the beast that continues to follow us daily like an angry hound, and to share how we manage to survive it one more day. It is therapeutic in important ways and should be spoken about more rather than less. Of course it is tiring to be in that conversation, but think about how tiring it is to be living the life that is being spoken about every day, from birth to death. If you are a white person who is wondering how you can be in solidarity with black people and other people of color, this is one of the first and most basic places where you can enter with your listening ear and heart. The willingness and ability to do that are a rare gift, because most whites seem unable to stay in the conversation for the long term.

I hasten to say that if you are white and cannot stay in the conversation, it is all right to stand where you can with integrity, because that is always the best place to be. But it will be helpful if you are able to understand the privilege and luxury that you have in being able to make such a choice, and if you can stay willing to own that space, it will still be helpful in advancing the work. Many whites are very quick to declare that they do not have privilege, but it is a major privilege to be able to move in and out of the racial healing arena as you see fit. That fact is neither negative nor positive; it simply is a fact. There is no judgment to be made in stating this fact, and actually no criticism—just simple acknowledgment of the truth. To allow the liberating energy created by this acknowledgment to become a part of the conversation can be a gift and can lead to healing.

When black, brown, and white people engage with one another, it's helpful to be as truthful as possible. While at times we may not know what the truth happens to be in that particular moment, it is important to work to find the space to allow for it to be revealed. Blacks and other people of color grow weary of whites who cannot see their privilege and consider that they should be exempt from anything beyond giving a cursory nod to racism. This type of unconsciousness is difficult to navigate and often leads people of color to the point of being unwilling to continue in the conversation or to make any effort at maintaining relationships.

Since I was a child in rural Arkansas—refusing to sit down in our doctor's segregated waiting room, always thinking that something was wrong in the little rural village where I lived without truly knowing what to call it—I have resisted racism and its intention to determine what my life could be. As I grew up and learned what racism was, I did not know what to do with that knowledge; I had no one in my family to shepherd me with it, for my parents were mostly interested in the daily tasks of trying to survive and provide for my siblings and me. When I got to college, I began to catch a glimpse of what to call it, though I still had a very small lens through which to view racism. In 1969, during my fourth year in college, a young boy was murdered by our campus's white security guard, and it was our student protest and undying devotion to the idea of resisting racism and its oppressive tendencies that helped to focus the lens much more clearly for me. It was during that time that my vocation for this work was clarified. I knew that I wanted to work in all the ways that were possible for me to make things better for myself, others like me, and everyone else. I am grateful that God has helped me to move to the space where I stand now and that from this space I can write this book and declare that everyone is a beloved child of God and should be treated as such.

Can you take a bit of time to reflect upon any conversations about race that you have had in the past, and how you found them? What is your response to the mention of race in everyday situations such as interactions between the police and people of color or people on the margin? Are you able to see how race intersects with most of our life experiences? Can you listen to conversations on race or engage in them without wishing or trying to change the subject? If you could frame a conversation on race around your deepest thoughts and feelings regarding it, how would it look? It would be good to spend a bit of your time with a journal when reflecting upon these questions, as well as with a therapist or spiritual director.

We have to do far more than talk about racism, but the work of transformation must engage conversation. Transformation cannot take place in a vacuum, but it can emerge even from relationships that are complicated and painful. And even situations that are disturbing and appear mostly negative can result in change, sometimes almost without being noticed. This is a good enough reason to work at finding the courage to stay in conversation with ourselves and others around race and its many challenging threads.

Part 4

WHAT'S LOVE GOT TO DO WITH RACIAL HEALING?

What Kind of Love Does It Take?

There is so much talk these days about love and how it is the remedy for what ails our society, and especially what ails our churches. But a serious problem with this talk is the lack of a clear definition of the word *love.* We use it to describe how we feel about our cat or dog and about the latest new shiny toy that we have purchased; when we begin to speak about racial wounds and other ills in our society, we say that we just need to love one another. It is necessary to examine the concept of love from several points of view and see if we can determine what it has to do with creating the space for racial healing and realizing beloved community in this lifetime.

One of the most powerful voices can be heard in 1 Corinthians where the writer declares, "Love is patient, love is kind. It does not envy, it does not boast, it is not proud. It does not dishonor others, it is not self-seeking, it is not easily angered, it keeps no record of wrongs. Love does not delight in evil but rejoices with the truth. It always protects, always trusts, always hopes, always perseveres. Love never fails" (1 Corinthians 13:4–8). Dr. Howard Thurman tells us that we need to live our lives by an ethical imperative that he calls the "Love Ethic," which demands that we see a person beyond all of their assets and deficits.[17] Both Thurman's words and 1 Corinthians offer a blueprint for how we might begin to explore what the concept means for us.

We use the term *love* thinking that everyone knows exactly what it means and are ready to govern themselves accordingly, though nothing could be further from the truth. This creates a wide gap that is not easy to bridge, and makes it harder to arrive at any agreed-upon place to begin to work for racial healing. When we are not careful enough about how we use language, the results will be less than satisfactory. We have been talking about love for eons and we have been trying to destabilize racism for about the same amount of time; yet consider the distance that remains to be traveled before we get to a common space of respect and care for one another.

The I Corinthians passage offers an amazingly beautiful and concrete summary of what love embodies. Along with that, it asks the reader to think seriously about whether that is what we actually desire. When we bring racism to the table in an effort to undo it, are we truly interested in love having anything to do with it? If so, what will our action be? Those who say that to fix racism "we just have to love one another" are asked by this passage to think about what that means. How do we imagine love when it comes to this issue?

The Love Ethic, which is clearly grounded in the same understanding of love as the writer of I Corinthians is imagining, tells us that we have to lay aside judgment and some of the negative and unproductive ways that we think about ourselves and others. It challenges us to reimagine who we are as humans who happen to have different skin colors rather than as black, brown, or white folks who cannot connect to one another. As a society, do we want to do that? Are we ready for the deep healing that would come to us if we decided to work to truly see God in everyone and to see their worthiness? It is quite challenging to think about what it means to leave aside people's assets and faults and how we might go about it. Do we have any models for beginning such work? Perhaps the best example can be found by observing children. They are so forgiving, especially of parents.

White people have a fair amount of work to do in forgiving themselves: for having white skin; for buying into the horrible construct of systemic racism and spending a good portion of their lives defending it, supporting it, trying to explain it, hating it, being ashamed of it, benefiting from it, exporting it, and doing everything in their power to justify it; and for blaming black and brown people when that system destroys their ability to see their agency and to navigate the soul-killing oppression it brings. Can the idea of love help here? Yes, it can, and it has when those who are searching have been willing to open their hearts and minds for this radically revolutionary energy to enter.

Black and brown people have to allow their hearts and minds to be open to the same type of radical internal reorganization. Racism has wounded them too, and those wounds have to be put into conversation with the energy of the Love Ethic in order for them to forgive themselves for any ways in which they have said yes to the seduction of systemic racism, something that happens every day. What false promises did it make to them, and what did they do with those promises? How do they engage the Love Ethic when it comes to whites and other people of color? How has racism kept them from fully realizing their own agency or lured them into exchanging their agency for the illusion of power? The verses of 1 Corinthians invite self-compassion and grace. Infusing the conversation with the Love Ethic changes the dynamic from one that supports polarizing energy to one that is willing to entertain the possibility of something being born between the groups coming together.

When we think deeply about this issue, we have to realize that it comes down to asking ourselves: Do we want to love this way? As white people, do we want to see the barriers broken down? Do we really want to cross the lines of difference and enter into relationships with people of color, walk alongside them, and embrace the suffering caused by the system undergirding our understanding of reality? As black and brown people, are we willing to take the chance that we can find genuine white people who are sincere about crossing the barriers? Can we trust that we can engage in such conversations without losing our sense of self in the process? Can the expression of love as it is described in I Corinthians and reaffirmed in Thurman's Love Ethic help us embrace and overcome the racialized trauma and continuing racist injury while we begin new conversations that might open the door for racial healing?

Drawing on love in the work of racial healing takes commitment and perseverance. No sound bite, press conference, book, speech, sermon, workshop, or webinar proclaiming that "love is the answer" will have any effect unless individual humans make the deep commitment at the core of their being to step onto the path and enter into the conversation with a fresh determination to be more open to this type of love.

MEDITATION 20

Whose Love is It, Anyway?

The previous meditation described a deep love given by Spirit in a way that takes one's breath away. This love challenges every fiber of a person's being because it cannot be achieved without action; it cannot be realized without the willingness to let go of old ways of being. It cannot be manufactured or manipulated; it requires a radical reorientation of the way one sees the world. It is deep and relentless in its intention to create something new.

This mystical love is not magic. It will not lend itself to the modern-day preoccupation that everything needs to happen instantaneously. It is the slow work of God and will be done on God's terms. It is through its slowness that it works; it does not allow humans' overzealousness to change its course. Its source is God and *Sophia* (Wisdom), and it comes to humans as a gift. It cannot be negotiated; it can only be accepted or rejected. One must welcome it without any expectation of managing it.

One of the main things that happens when humans allow themselves to step into the energy of this love is disruption. Its promise to disrupt the status quo is the main reason this type of love is not as welcome as it should be. It was the encounter with this kind of love that led Mahalia Jackson to declare in a song, "I told Jesus he could change my name." It has that type of force. It makes it possible for humans to stretch far beyond what they might have imagined before the encounter. It helps to solidify a new way to see and to be.

This is not love that is interested in how you feel about clothing, food, sunsets, the ocean, or music. It transcends ego. Its aim is the radical reorganization of the inner community, making possible the internal changes that give us the energy to change the outer world. Systemic racism cannot survive this type of destabilization and will fight to resist it. But the human commitment to the journey is all that is necessary to set this love free to do its work.

Do you have a memory of an encounter with such love? If not, is it the type of love that you are hoping to encounter on this pilgrim journey?

When someone proclaims "Love is the answer," pay attention to the kind of love they're talking about. If this is a statement about some kind of warm and fuzzy niceness, discard it quickly. But if it is an affirmation of the love that is rooted in God and *Sophia* (Wisdom), which calls us to go beyond the safety of the ego into the depths of one's soul, it is the kind of love that we need for healing work. This love is not given by the world, and the world cannot take it away. While it often leads to something that feels like dying, in truth it brings abundant life. It brings healing.

MEDITATION 21

Is There Any Love Here?

Songwriters and poets often ask, "Where is the love?" We can hope that most of the time the answer is "Not too far away." But when we spend any time reflecting on that question, we begin to wonder, especially when we assess the brokenness in our culture around race relations.

Perhaps the most confusing places to find a lack of love is in our faith communities. We have high expectations of finding love there, because the people who make up those communities label themselves as people who love one another. Unfortunately, there is often a very large chasm between the proclamation about being a loving community and actually being one.

If a community wishes to declare itself a place that exemplifies the love spoken about in the previous meditation, it will have to become a place that is ready to defy the status quo and allow itself to be a disrupter. It cannot hold allegiance to anything except the commitment to embrace whomever it encounters as they are encountered. Such a community spends no energy trying to remake people to fit its standards. It does not apologize for cultural constructs that restrict freedom. It has no patience with anything that does not bear witness to life and the intention to experience life fully.

But as one moves across our land, it is far too easy to find communities that struggle with this type of love or even embrace its opposite. Faith communities and other spaces that seek to nurture such radical love must boldly block the path of racism and proclaim it as a way not to follow. While such communities would not exclude any person seeking to be loved, no matter what that individual's present state of being, they would make it quite clear that racism is not welcome in their space. Any community that would tolerate the unwillingness to love another person simply because of the color of their skin is not a true community of love, not a true space of bravery. And any community that claims to be a brave space or a faith community yet fails to stand against the denigration and dehumanization of anyone is untrustworthy. There are many ways in which a community of faith can declare its lack of love, and such places create pain and suffering. Sometimes a congregation appears to be loving until we connect with it and learn who they really are and what is truly important to them. We simply have to learn how to discern the best places for us to land.

Combating racism takes more than just being nice. An indefensible system such as racism cannot be tweaked a bit and made palatable by folks who are trying very hard to be nice. The mystical love of I Corinthians demands action as well as being. And it demands truth-telling. We need to find spaces where the truth will be told consistently and where the members of the community are not encouraged to look for the easiest way out of every situation. It is important to understand that when telling the truth, one does not have to tell everything that one knows. But there has to be a basic commitment to telling the best truth possible no matter where it might lead.

Spaces that are not very committed to truth-telling are not generally filled with love; they usually feel more like transactional places. There is not much commitment to the inner journey because that work does not fit their intention in the world. Often what they are seeking is behavioral prescriptions, instead of connection with the radical otherness of Spirit. Racism can find a comfortable home in spaces like these. When they are predominantly communities of color, they are challenged with the wounds of racialized trauma and colorism, the preoccupation with skin color and hair textures and their members easily slide into defensively othering anyone who is outside of that group, such as unsheltered people, and even some in their own group. Their major problem-solving remedy is projection, because it is easier than taking personal responsibility to make changes.

If we encounter unloving spaces, we must feel free to vacate them without being apologetic about it. It can be challenging to embrace the discernment process quickly and without a sense of guilt or shame, but when it is clear that the existing energy in a space mitigates against life, it is against God, and so it is reasonable to seek a more life-giving space.

These questions are good to ponder as we reflect upon the quality of the spaces that we have encountered in the search of community.

Do you find it easy to discern when a space needs to be vacated? How do you vacate such spaces with love in spite of the fact that you did not find them to be loving? What did the process teach you about boundaries and how did it assist you with your racial healing efforts?

MEDITATION 22

Stop Talking Until You Have Love

"I don't see color." This is one of the most unfortunate comments that a white person can make when speaking about a person of color. The words are insulting no matter how they are intended. For one thing, they are not true: there is no way not to see the color of someone's skin when standing in front of them. What point is such a declaration actually trying to make? And is there a better way to make that point, whatever it happens to be?

In an effort to be fair-minded in thinking about this, I have concluded that for the most part such comments are an attempt to communicate a willingness to see beyond color. That's admirable, but proclaiming not to see color does not get that point across very well. White people who are determined to confront racism in the outer world and in their inner world need to reflect deeply upon what it means to declare such a position. One's skin color happens to matter in a land that is stratified on race. So to declare that you do not see that color is not a compliment but a denigration. It says, *I will not take into consideration your experience as a person living in that body with that skin, and I will assign you whatever is being assigned to help me in navigating this space with you.* There is a definite arrogance inherent in this declaration that is actually proclaiming an intention to see persons of color as they imagine them rather than as they are.

There can never be a positive outcome from saying "I don't see skin color." It is a denial of a very important part of the person, and it makes it difficult to develop any type of relationship that is grounded in the truth of who both parties happen to be.

What does love to have to do with this dilemma? Love can assist you in developing better listening skills as you travel on the path to deeper consciousness. While it cannot save you from every pitfall, it can help in creating the space that allows you to wonder more deeply about what is best to say and what is best left unsaid. It can help in the process of reflecting on how certain things might be understood by another person, especially a person of color regarding race.

The idea of love that 1 Corinthians 13 describes offers the challenge to stay close to one's heart when thinking about another person and the way you treat them as a fellow pilgrim on the journey of life. It's not likely that all of us can live all the attributes listed in those verses, but simply reflecting upon them is humbling, and it can be helpful in thinking about how to be with others in the world. Those words are powerful enough to create a silence in the soul—a silence that makes one want to simply observe, rather than attempt to know what to say and when to say it. There are times when silence is one of the best gifts that can be given.

It would change the world if all of us could observe the deep messages found in 1 Corinthians' words about love, and practice Thurman's ethic of seeing people as beloved children of the Creator, no matter what their assets or deficits. But no matter how hard we try, humans have a recurring psychological urge to seek to know more than we can know, and when we encounter a lack of information, we fill in the blanks as best we can. That's when projection and all of its little minions come to the forefront. When we encounter new people, and especially when there are racial differences, we feel a powerful impetus to fill in the blanks with projected information. However, practicing love and kindness can help us to keep our mouths closed until we have more and often better information about a person or a situation. It is a good idea to ask ourselves if speaking will improve on silence; if not, then staying quiet is a great idea.

MEDITATION 23

No Cheap Love, Please

What does cheap love look like? We could probably call it by many other names, but it's what allows people of color and white people to sit in pews together for decades and know nothing about one another. It affirms that surface relationships will suffice. So we occupy physical space together and talk about how much we love one another, yet we never share our deepest hopes and fears.

I saw a vivid example of this when I met with a lovely group of folks working in their church parish on race relations. As the conversation evolved, the white members voiced their concern about not knowing black people. I asked about their interactions with the four or five black people who had been a part of that parish community for decades, and learned that despite the years that they had been together, they had all allowed their relationships to stay at a very surface level. This is a tragic situation, but I know that it is not uncommon. We talk about a parish being diverse if there is a handful of people of color in it, but the challenges of racism do not allow them to have a truly loving diverse community.

I agree that proximity is a critical factor in the process of racial healing, but it has to be partnered with truth-telling, which does not happen simply because the space is shared—and, of course, it cannot happen at all if there is no proximity. This dynamic is much like talking about love itself, as we discussed in an earlier meditation. When we proclaim that we can solve our problems by loving everyone, that happens to be true, but it takes so much more than having superficial conversations during the parish coffee hour. Our culture encourages us to stay shallow as we rush past one another in the busy-ness of life, and that attitude is a major detriment if we are striving to develop a deeper level of community.

Great frustration is generated in spaces where there is constant talk about how much love is present but no depth of relationship between the people talking. It takes more than learning how to be good at transactional relating to make a healing community, much less a beloved community. When white people believe that they know a lot about black people and other people of color, they need to check that out with the people they are in relationships with (when it is appropriate). But it is also possible to check it out by doing a bit of self-inventory. What is your response to situations such as uncalled-for killings by police officers of black and brown folks? What do you think when you see a person of color who is living without shelter and asking for assistance? What do you project onto the young black mother with three or four small children in the grocery store shopping with food stamps?

It is important not to make the folks that you sit in the pew with the "exceptional Negro." And while there is no mandate that requires you to go out and make friends with the person sleeping under the bridge, there is something to be said about the way that person is perceived and the amount of I Corinthians 13 love that is available to them as well as to your pew-mate. This matter of love being grounded deeply below the surface so that it can stand the tests of struggle and time is complicated, and deserving of deep and serious reflection.

People of color have their challenges with this issue as well. It is easy enough to wear the mask. The culture has taught black people in particular, and more than likely all people of color, that mask-wearing in predominantly white spaces is the best policy for ensuring survival. I grew up hearing this wise old saying that had been around for years: "When someone white asks you where you are going, tell them where you have been; when they ask where you have been, tell them where you are going. You are talking all the time and they are not getting any true information." Deceit and love do not go together very well, but such a strategy helps protect you from being harmed by the enemy. It is difficult for black people to get beyond seeing whites as the enemy; making that journey is totally dependent upon the mystical love that goes to the depths of the soul in a way that makes it impossible not to be genuine. Cultural memory bears witness to the fact that there is no reason to be trusting of the person standing in front of you in white skin, yet the church community says, "We are here together because we love one another, because we call this church and that is the way it is supposed to be." The struggle people of color experience is totally justified, but the silence that surrounds it within the community makes it tragic.

When a community, regardless of whether it is called church or something else, refuses to allow that struggle to be named and proceeds to build a life together on the lie that they love one another, even though they don't know anything about one another and don't trust one another, it is not possible for the healing light of true consciousness to shine in that space. When whites are not honest about where they really are, and when both white people and people of color live in a world of agreed-upon conspiracies of silence about what is really important in their lives, we have what confronts us today: a lot of rhetoric about beloved community and love, but no true opportunities for the authentic community and deep healing that can help dismantle racism.

Cheap love makes a transactional attitude seem appropriate. But healing does not occur through transactional relating. True healing comes about when struggle disrupts the ego so that it cannot go back to the status quo. Of course, maintaining the status quo is exactly what a transactional attitude is after in the first place: to do enough so that it appears that everything is fine, but stay close enough to the surface so that things don't get messy. The work of creating space for the love that truly heals is messy and disruptive, and when those encounters occur, none of the participants will ever be the same.

This love creates metanoia, a new way to behave, and it is profound enough to create the sense of having a new name. The old ways of being are removed so that God's and Sophia's gift of mystical love can be accepted.

What would it be like for this type of transforming energy of love to change your name? Can you imagine that for yourself?

MEDITATION 24

Reimagining Love and Racial Healing

Regardless of skin color or station in life, we are all challenged to be loving toward one another. But in the case of black people as well as other people of color, the large gap between them and whites has made that seem impossible. One part of the challenge to the development of loving relationships across racial lines lies in the fact that there never has been an opportunity for blacks to enter into that process freely. The mandate to act loving and to be forgiving was a precondition for having even the smallest degree of success or acceptance in a racialized society. Blacks had to make sure to be careful not to demonstrate too much dissatisfaction with white behavior, no matter what shape it took.

The most vivid recent demonstration of this was the 2015 massacre at Mother Emanuel Church in Charleston, South Carolina. As most readers are likely to recall, Dylann Roof entered the Wednesday evening Bible study there with the intention of murdering people, and he killed nine. While the entire country was reeling from the horror and shock of that news, some of the victims' family members were voicing words about forgiveness, which carried the implication that they were responding in love.

I recall listening to those lovely words proclaiming a readiness to be forgiving, and reflecting on how hollow they sounded in the midst of such horror. But blacks have been taught that the best response to all white behavior is to try taking what we like to believe is the "high road." While that is a noble notion, it is not a reflection of the way people navigating such horrors will get to forgiveness. The kind of love described in 1 Corinthians 13 will be the only kind to aid in making forgiveness possible and it will not be manifested magically, as it might have seemed when listening to the victims' family members at Mother Emanuel.

An unfortunate historical narrative has fostered the notion that rage and outrage would have been too much, even as a response to such evil—that black people cannot ever demonstrate that level of disapproval of white behavior. Of course, historically, when blacks were dependent for their livelihood on whites, it made sense to be careful about how we responded to acts of denigration and violence, lest those responses generate more violence—as happened in 1912 when the black community of Forsyth County, Georgia, was destroyed by whites responding to the accusation of rape and murder of a white woman by a black man.[18] These acts of terror in response to blacks being willing to tell the truth about their feelings taught them to stop doing it.

Thus, as I listened to the beautiful voices of these family members proclaiming their willingness to forgive Roof the day after the massacre, I had a deep desire to hear them say what they were really feeling. But the shock and horror, the grief and the rage and the sense of helplessness—all of that was pushed down so that the white community could hear what it wanted to hear: blacks being strong, speaking about forgiving, and stepping up to accommodate white violence one more time.

Whites can help to create space for liberating love by allowing that same love energy to give them the courage to hear whatever black and brown people need to say. "Tell me your truth and I will listen as best I can," they can say, and that invitation will become a light to illuminate the path toward the mystical love that this section has been exploring. And when that invitation is extended, it is important for it to be accepted. While there are still a lot of possible negative repercussions for blacks who tell their truth whether whites like it or not, it is not as dangerous as it was decades ago.

Black and brown people will have to take the initiative to move this process into a different space, but many of them have concluded that it is a lost cause; they do not see much reason to believe that whites are genuinely interested in developing such relationships. This conclusion is problematic, because it negatively impacts personal healing journeys. But many black and brown people simply are not willing to take the chance that they will be victimized again by racism if they venture into this process of reimagining love.

The invitation to step into the arena where the healing light shines more brightly remains available to everyone, and the hope is that each day will bring all of us closer to having the capacity to say yes. A few steps onto the path where courage resides will enlarge that capacity, and the personal liberation it brings makes it worth the risk. All racial healing work needs to be designed to help make that path wider and easier for all—black, white, and brown—to traverse.

Part 5

GOING BELOW THE SURFACE AND CREATING NEW SPACE FOR HEALING

MEDITATION 25

No Trespassing

I was the only African American staff member at the Macon-Bibb County Mental Health Center in 1973. I learned a lot during my time there, and it has taken me almost fifty years to decipher some of those lessons. I learned lessons about white women that I have come to understand much better now than I did at that time.

One day all of the white women and I were in the lounge discussing where to go to lunch. A senior member of the staff suggested her club. The others agreed, but as they got up to leave, I did not move. One of them turned back to me and said, "Aren't you coming?" The staff member who had made the suggestion replied, "She can't come. They don't let black folks come there." They all departed for lunch, leaving me sitting there. When they returned, I felt certain that at least one of them would apologize or at least acknowledge that it was unfortunate that another suggestion for lunch had not been made so that I could've participated. But no one ever said a word. Yet several of those women acted as if they were my friends, and I thought they were; one of them went so far as to purchase the same type of skin care products that I used because she thought my skin looked so healthy.

Now, I realize that this behavior was another example of how too many white women have betrayed black women's idea that they were friends who would stand with them in times of trouble and stand up for them in general. Many decades of study and interrogation of racial issues in America and my deep sense of commitment to work for racial healing have led me to stay reflective about this tangled web and have forced me to search for ways to talk about it.

As I learn more about archetypal wounding, grieving, and ancestral memory being passed along from generation to generation, I see how the sense of betrayal that women of color have in regard to white women's overtures of friendship reflects our history. Because white women often claimed that our enslaved foremothers and foresisters were important to them, those black women must have wondered why the white women did not come to their rescue when they were being raped and dehumanized by white men.

Along with this, I think about the white women who have told me how important their black maids were to them; some have proclaimed them to be their best friends. But recall how many of these maids worked long hours, taking them away from their children and other family members. The white women seemed to have no concern about imagining ways to manage a bit differently so their "best friend" could finish her work and get home at a reasonable time to see about her own family.

This disregard has continued into the twenty-first century. I hear many horror stories of betrayal by white women who have professed friendship with black women, but when the time arrives to stand up for their "friend" in the face of abuse, they cannot be found. Yet many white women seem to enjoy being around black women, and many praise them incessantly for being strong, resilient, and able to navigate so much struggle and pain. They seem to have little or no ability to see black women as people like themselves, who need and wish to have less struggle and pain.

Recently a white woman friend of fifty years helped me to name this pattern of behavior as *trespassing*—coming into someone's space to take what you like. In this context it involves attempting to model your life on some aspect of their life without deeply appreciating and caring about them. I've come to think of this as white women trespassing in black women's soul gardens—picking the flowers from those gardens, putting them in their houses, and then calling black women in to admire those flowers as if the white women grew them themselves. In the 1960s there was much talk about this issue in regard to black men connecting to white women, as I mentioned earlier; while many professional black women were troubled by this phenomenon, thinking that the white women were just after the men, in fact they may have been after the soul force they saw in black women. If so, it would have been far better for them to connect to the women directly, bringing what they have to give and seeing what black women wish to give freely.

It is possible for white women and black women to have honest and authentic relationships if and when white women are willing to tell their truth and admit to their envy, jealousy, admiration, and often fear of black women. They need to stop carrying on about the strength of black women and admit to their own sense of weakness, which in some ways seems to immobilize them in terms of addressing their personal racism. If they are willing to be vulnerable, admit that they are in search of healing and empowerment, and acknowledge that they think black women can help them, that can lead to new energy.

MEDITATION 26

Invisibility Blues

" . . . And ain't I a woman?" asked Sojourner Truth all those years ago when she was trying to make sense out of experiencing invisibility. In a culture constructed upon the premise that the Black woman is basically the mule of the world whose job is to pick up whatever is thrown down before her and to make the best of it, as Zora Neale Hurston's character Janie affirms in *Their Eyes Were Watching God*, "the black woman is the mule of the world."[19]

In the previous meditation, I shared a story about being made invisible by a group of white women colleagues. Until I wrote it down, it had been decades since I thought about that incident, and exposing it here led me to relive some of the pain of it. But I realized that now I can confront that soul-wrenching pain, when I have so much confidence that I am living the life that I came here to live. For the first time, I have the clarity to see that pain and the language to describe it.

Part of the reason that the group of co-workers who went off to the whites-only club without me did not feel the necessity to speak about it ever again lies in the fact that I was invisible to them in many ways. From that point of view, they weren't leaving anybody behind. Of course, none of them would have been able to name what was actually happening. This conclusion arises out of my belief that no one who was conscious of me as an equal human being would have been willing to treat me in that manner. They did not see the part of me that was like themselves, the part that would be hurt by such treatment.

There is a complex set of dynamics that need to be interrogated by white women to make deep and sustainable relationships with black women possible. While there are some instances of such relationships in the present moment, we need them to become much more widespread in order to create the healing energy necessary to destabilize systemic racism.

Racism has wounded everyone in this country; there is no escaping that reality. But when you are a white person, talking of color-blindness or describing an injustice against you in order to show your solidarity with a black person who has shared a situation that represents a lifetime of trespassing and invisibility is insulting and hurtful. While a white person may surely tell their story of being wronged and deserves to be heard with a compassionate heart, telling a story of one event of denigration in response to what a black person has said about a lifetime of denigration is akin to someone who has lost a fingernail sharing that loss with a person who has lost a hand in an effort to show empathy and solidarity; the intention may be a good one, but the behavior is not helpful.

Nor should stories be edited or diminished so that the hearers will feel less discomfort. We need to tell the best truth possible. Black women are well versed in the "do not make white people feel too bad or scared" narrative, in order to manage white women's fragility, fear, and inability to stay in the pain of creation until something is born, but it is time to vacate that position. The conversation is critical, and the energy around the awakening will be troublesome until it isn't.

For women of color, awakening to the necessity to do this work is painful, risky, and fear-inducing. When we realize that we have to stay open to healing in spite of the depths of the wounds caused by racialized trauma, we soon learn that it will cost us everything to do so. But all of us are called to do our part. Let's be a half shade braver.

MEDITATION 27

Looking for More than an Ally

Ponder this: If you were dying, who would you prefer to be accompanying you on the journey—an ally or a fellow pilgrim?

A fellow pilgrim is one who holds you in their heart and shares your pain and joy to the very best of their ability, no matter what it requires. This person is willing to walk in your shoes in order to understand how you see the world. The fellow pilgrim's commitment is to hold the difficult, regardless of what it costs to do so. There is no thought of abandoning the relationship, because it is clearly a connection at the soul level, and it will not be broken by external circumstances that might cause inconvenience.

The ally is quite a bit different. Allies have decided to unite with those in some type of struggle, and they have a variety of reasons for doing so. They will be present to the particular portion of the struggle that called them into it, but there may not be a soul-deep commitment that is grounded in true empathy. That empathy and commitment are essential to help create a space for sustainable racial healing.

While it is difficult to know or judge the exact process a person follows to arrive at a particular place in their life, clearly the process of deciding to be an ally is vastly different from that of deciding to be a fellow pilgrim. In my experience, it has seemed that becoming an ally is more grounded in the energy of transaction than transformation. But pilgrims take that next step. White people who have come to realize that racism has injured not only black and brown people but themselves as well are becoming aware of their personal need for healing. In these cases, the active pursuit of a deep consciousness can spark an awareness that the work is not simply about standing with a person of color in a protest or an effort to achieve a particular justice-making goal, but also about getting well themselves.

The profound understanding of shared sickness when it comes to racism is the first step in the process of becoming a fellow pilgrim. We all are injured by racism. The great pilgrim Howard Thurman declared that "when we are giving to others, it is important to understand that we are working to get ourselves out of prison."[20] But it is difficult to come to that understanding if we have not yet realized that we are no better off than those to whom we offer our assistance. Even though we may have a few more economic resources, we share being impoverished in all of the other ways that human beings can be impoverished. As we embrace that reality, we can begin the journey toward liberation and healing, because giving generously requires being willing to move out of our comfort zone and try to respond to the real needs of the ones receiving our gifts.

When it comes to racism, too many whites find it difficult to see how racism has injured them. Their involvement in racial healing work is purely outer-directed, focused on people of color, who are deemed to be the only victims of this horrid system. If you accept that every person on the planet is injured by racism, you can see that it causes separation from other humans in a way that makes it quite difficult to see the face of God in one another, and that results in psychic and spiritual injury. No one is immune. Opening our hearts and heads to this awareness, though painful, allows us entry into the arena of community as fellow pilgrims.

Being a pilgrim requires being willing to let go of privilege and many of the benefits of being white in the world. It means being more interested in being well than in being white. It requires white people to be willing to be uncomfortable as they observe the ways in which people of color and especially African Americans are treated. Being connected to people of color in that way creates pain for white people. There are times when sacrifices of white privilege will be called for in order to stand in solidarity as fellow pilgrims instead of being able to simply choose otherwise. There are times when the sense of security that accompanies white privilege may be diminished because a white person is deemed "less than" for standing with those who have long been characterized that way.

In order for white people to become fellow pilgrims, people of color have to be willing to allow them to enter into that space with them. This does not always happen, nor is it ever easy. It is difficult for many people of color to imagine themselves being truly connected to a white person because of the shared history that we collectively inhabit and the ways in which that history continues to shape the present. And there's not a lot of evidence that the vulnerability involved in taking off one's shoes to allow a white person to step into them is worth the risks involved.

When I went to Pepperdine University in 1968 as a young black woman who was not convinced that she would survive college or living in Los Angeles, I met the four white people I spoke about earlier who taught me the difference between a fellow pilgrim and an ally. These folks were student life personnel at the university, and they were prepared to go many extra miles with me and other students of color. This was during the era of student protest and efforts to hold institutions accountable for their behavior. It was refreshing to find honest people who did not seem to think that I needed to be anybody except who I was. They were accepting of me, and they extended many acts of kindness toward me. I had never met or known any white people like them. They were courageous, willing to risk loss for my sake and the sake of the other African American students on campus.

I had no background with whites that could have helped me to understand these folks. They were white, but they were consistently the same every time I had any type of interactions with them. They made it clear in multiple ways that my well-being mattered to them, but this was not a case of selecting me as the "designated negro" to receive their graciousness; they were caring toward everyone, and they were willing to stand up for any and all of us who were trying to claim our rights as humans living in brown and black bodies. They demonstrated love as described in 1 Corinthians 13, but I did not realize that at the time. Back then, I was not able to think about race in relation to myself in the ways that I have come to understand that part of my journey now; on most days, I was simply trying to keep up with my classes, work, and family.

Reflection about the group I had encountered would come later, after their way of being proved consistent as the years passed, affirming them as people who were not simply stepping in and out of racial justice arenas when it was convenient; they stayed faithful, standing against racism wherever they found it. They remained supporters and mentors for more than fifty years, and they never wavered from being totally committed to wanting my life to be the best that it could be. They were fellow pilgrims; these are the folks that I want in the room with me on my day of dying.

Do you have fellow pilgrims on the journey with you? Are you aspiring to be a pilgrim or an ally?

Trust

A few meditations ago, I wrote about the old wise black person's formula for survival: "When someone white asks you where you are going, tell them where you have been; when they ask where you have been, tell them where you are going. You are talking all the time and they are not getting any true information." Other things I heard in my youth included "I don't trust whites as far as I can throw them" and "Don't trust whites because as soon as someone white comes along and they need to stand with that person, they will be gone." I heard this philosophy in many places: the barbershop, the church, the schoolhouse, and my house. It was and continues to be grounded in the experiences of people of color.

The long lists of historical betrayals and day-to-day microaggressions continue to plague the efforts of any black, brown, or white person who is contemplating the journey from racial polarization to interracial community-building. These are undeniable realities, and it is impossible to act as if they are not a part of the challenge to open one's heart and invite in folks across racial lines. While it's prudent not to be hasty when building bridges across racial lines, it's good to remember that keeping an open heart is the only pathway to a life of peaceful contentment.

We are on this earth together, and it seems we have a choice: learn to live together, or continue to destroy one another. And we need to ground ourselves more deeply in this fact as we reflect upon our propensity for violence toward one another. Everyone on the planet has a part to play in this great dance of becoming human enough to live here in peace. It requires that we begin to imagine a new light that shines on us and allows us to see one another better. But how do we even begin when the darkness is so thick and there appears to be no light to be found? There are days when all who engage this work are tempted to find a safe corner and retreat there for the rest of time, but that is not an option: the planet cannot afford to lose the workforce that is committed to challenging racism's status quo. The energy that allows someone to say yes to the invitation to trust persons of a different color, to take a chance on them, lies deep in the heart, and it is there that the work begins.

It is easy to hide behind human constructs such as academic canons, the customs in our communities and families, religious orthodoxy, and the many other fronts designed to give racism a cover of credibility. Indeed, there are times when these constructs are so tightly bound to our sense of self that people of color as well as whites will furiously oppose attempts to bring them to the light. But as we work to identify the places that encourage us to remain unconscious, our hearts catch a glimpse of what it's like to be more open and trusting. Hearts would rather be open than closed; closed hearts lead to spiritual and psychological death. We were not meant to live in the polarizing ways that we have allowed ourselves to embrace. We must be willing to take a good look at those choices, explore why we think them to be necessary, and uncover what we are refusing to see.

At times it is difficult to believe that there is any connection between us, any reason to trust. For instance, I hear many young people of color proclaim quite clearly that they are not here to help whites save themselves or teach them how to become a fellow pilgrim, or anything else, for that matter. They have invested a fair amount of energy in the notion that we are all separate and can make it just fine as individuals; we figure out what works best for us and then move along. But we must break the cycle of superficial transactions and the diminishment of trust in one another. The heart knows this, but the journey from the head to the heart is a fairly long one and cannot be done without consent. The consent comes from within, and it's not always clear what triggers it. As each person walks on their daily path, they will respond as they can and in the ways that make the most sense for their particular set of circumstances.

The initial desire to move along the path to opening the heart does not have to be very large, but it has to be born through finding the courage to take a first step. Hopefully each time a heart becomes willing to take a step toward trust, there will be another person whose heart says, "I want to be free as well." That is the purpose of our work together: so that liberation makes more sense than bondage.

It takes massive amounts of energy to keep us away from one another, and how pitiful to do it primarily because our skin is a different color. There is much to be said for coming to understand that taking another look at race, no matter our skin color, is connected to the process of finding the path to contentment. No one is exempt. We don't have to foolishly go looking to befriend every person we can find who represents difference, but we do need to be willing to explore and reconcile the notion of the "other," however we define that, in all of the ways that make sense for each of us.

What circumstances need to change in order for you to say yes to the invitation to open your heart to someone in a group that differs from your group of origin? How do internal shifts affect this process? What fears do you have around trust? Are those fears justified by your personal experience or based in memory or stories that you have been told? What does your heart know? What does your heart want?

The books, the workshops, the classes, the pilgrimages, the films, the discussion groups, the speeches, the retreats, the counseling—all of these ways that we have devised to speak about racism and racial healing cannot give us the gift of trust. Trust arrives when least expected and disrupts the intention and effort to stay unconscious. It will not be controlled by cultural narratives that say no. It will work very diligently to lead us onto better paths toward healing if we have the desire to go there.

MEDITATION 29

Visibility

A part of the work for black people and other people of color involves making the unapologetic declaration "I am here with the intention to become the person that I was sent here to become." My father, who could neither read nor write, proclaimed, "I can cover the ground I stand on," but I am not sure that he really believed he could. He died at age seventy, partially from a broken heart about never being able to rise above blackness and poverty. But I heard him, and I embodied that message without realizing it until I was much older and able to investigate the threads of my life in ways that helped me to arrive where I am today: a place of seeing the way much better.

"I can cover the ground that I stand on as I decide when and how to enter the arena and become the person that the Creator had in mind in putting me on the earth," a person of any color might proclaim in the face of the arrogance of white expressions of superiority. It can be daunting to encounter that attitude, which is found so often in the white community and reflects a sense of owning the world. White people need to note that it is not simple to keep one's focus and continue to make the effort to engage with them in the face of such expressions, but relenting is not an option. The continuing intention to move forward has to be grounded in something other than simply railing against whiteness; it's necessary to discover at one's core why it is important to stay on this path. What is the call from the heart to keep saying yes? There has to be some sense of a larger purpose that propels the journey. Many people of color simply cannot make the trip because the circumstances of their lives will not support it.

The journey to visibility, the willingness to show up in the world in the way that you believe to be the best for you, can be challenging, and it can become tempting to turn away from it when there is criticism from many directions, including your own head. I recall those voices of criticism not only being in my head but also coming from my family and my teachers, who would say disparaging things designed to short-circuit my willingness to imagine for myself what they could not see for me or for themselves. Some of it may have been the result of their fear that I would be disappointed in my aspirations, but they did not know that they would simply have to allow me to take that chance. It was my life and not theirs.

When I was in the seventh grade, I proclaimed very proudly that I was going to run for president of the United States someday. I was thirteen years old, and to this day I remember my teacher saying, "Well, you must be planning to stay single for the rest of your life if you want to do all that kind of thing." Oh, my—what a way to try to stop a teenage girl from dreaming and thinking out loud about being more visible in the world. I'm so glad that there was something in me that wondered why she thought that way. Of course, hearing that from her helped prepare me for the thousands of ways the same message would be directed at me as I moved into the larger world.

Another quite vivid memory is of a white woman colleague who took the liberty of telling me, "You are a person who is achievement-oriented," with a sneer that made that it sound like a dread disease or something to be avoided at all costs. She must not have thought that being achievement-oriented was the worst thing that could happen to anyone, because she went on to graduate school and eventually completed her doctoral degree. But there was something about watching a young black woman aspire that was troubling to her and led her to make such an overly critical evaluation.

Often whites have made it clear that my way of being outspoken, clearheaded, honest, passionate, and self-assured, able to express anger without apologizing for it or being intimated by the label "angry black woman," causes problems and sometimes fear for them. This type of unconsciousness is why many blacks and perhaps other people of color decide that there is no use in trying to form relationships with whites; why seek out folks who respond that way to their efforts to become the person that their souls seek to be? It is tiring, to say the least. And it is tempting to take steps to protect oneself from the possibility of such racist and injurious characterizations.

But such efforts at self-protection result in being closed to the warmth of relationship in general and specifically to the possibility of missing the gift of true friendship, as I have found with a small group of white people who work diligently to be conscious. These are fellow pilgrims who are committed to laying their lives down for me and other people of color if need be. They are not people who only have one black or brown friend and walk through life thinking that to be sufficient evidence that they have worked out racism for themselves. I am glad that there was something set free in my little Arkansas sharecropper's daughter's hungry heart that said, "I will look for the truth everywhere and will not allow unconscious, racist whites deter me from that task. I will not allow them to control my behavior. And I will not allow myself to hate them because that would be giving them power they do not deserve to have." The inner drive to find out who I am intended to be—to learn what mark was placed on my heart as I was being sent to earth—is greater than racism and stronger than any effort to deter or manage me. Visibility, showing up in the world as if I belong here, is the task that was and continues to be mine to complete.

It took a long time for this message to become clearer to me. Even though I spoke up some as a youngster and then in college, I think my voice was tentative during those early years; it was difficult to be as certain then as I am today of the possibility of living the life that I was sent to the earth to live. And when that self-knowledge meets racism, it shakes racism to the core.

Efforts to prevent the visibility of people deemed to be "other" in some way are not confined to race alone, but they are especially problematic in the racial healing arena. Such efforts have to be resisted, defied, and eventually sent away by vigilant determination to be visible. There is no negotiating with this type of negative energy; we must make it clear that it will not be allowed to live in our inner or outer community. The morning light must shine on it until it is transformed into the power that moves us to stand taller and to be as visible as possible.

MEDITATION 30

Don't Get Too Weary

persevere: to persist in a state, enterprise, or undertaking in spite of counterinfluences, opposition, or discouragement.

—*Merriam-Webster.com Dictionary*

It was inspiring to listen to a recap of the highlights from Supreme Court nominee Ketanji Brown Jackson's Senate confirmation hearing in the spring of 2022. I heard her tell the story of being a first-year student at Harvard who had come from very humble beginnings with no real preparation for being in that environment except a stellar intellect and a spirit of determination. She shared that she had much fear about being able to survive in that environment. One day while walking on campus, she encountered an African American woman who, she imagined, picked up on her sense of lostness and said to her, "Persevere," as she walked past her. That word stayed with her, and now she advises young people who seek counsel from her to do the same thing. This is a good word for all of us to ponder.

I also watched Senator Cory Booker's impassioned speech paying tribute to Judge Brown and the late Judge Constance Baker Motley, the first black woman to argue before the Supreme Court, to be appointed a federal judge, and to be elected to the New York State Senate. Judge Jackson's story and Senator Booker's tribute were the only reasons to listen to what happened in the hearing room. It has been said that Judge Jackson is one of the best-qualified candidates who has ever been presented for appointment to the high honor of sitting on the Supreme Court, but a great amount of what happened in the Judiciary Committee hearing involved disrespectful posturing by some white men who appeared to be grown-ups but sounded and behaved more like teenage boys trying to see which one of them could win the bad-boy contest than like colleagues showing respect for her record and intellect.

It is a bit difficult to understand what would make people who hold the title of senator decide to demean that title and what their oath of office calls them to do by behaving like empty-headed schoolyard bullies. But part of the answer is that she is an African American woman and they are white men who appear to still be living in the unconsciousness of yesteryear. It appears that they are holding on to the notion that one needs to do everything possible to discredit African American excellence, integrity, and commitment to the ideals upon which this country was founded, and to block an African American woman from having a seat at one of our highest tables. I wonder if they are conscious enough to know what they really did that week.

Still, all of us, regardless of race, class, or gender, can be proud to be present in this moment, when we have the chance to bear witness to what happens when a little African American girl dares to believe that this land belongs to her and that she can use her intellect and skills to be a free woman someday. She sat in that seat during the hearings for all of us who understand what it is like to be marginalized, denigrated, and deemed unworthy for one reason and one reason only: because we are not white. Had she a white skin, this woman would have been treated far differently than she was.

But she rose to the occasion and did not allow their racist disrespect to destabilize her. She remained calm, clear-headed, poised, and grounded in an understanding of who she is and her place on this planet and in this country. Knowing how to persevere in the face of adversity and in the face of schoolyard bullying, she made all of us who care about being good human beings proud. She modeled for us how to be visible by persevering, and all of us can learn from her stellar example.

Judge Jackson's treatment provides a profound opportunity to reflect on all the things that have been discussed in this section: trespassing, invisibility, trust, visibility, and not growing too weary. She embodied all of that for the world to witness as she sat there during those hearings and persevered. She gave us a gift, and all who care to see it can learn from it, no matter what your skin color.

Of course, if you choose to work on explaining those wrongs, making excuses for them, or finding ways to justify any of them, that presents a completely different set of challenges for you to face. It is not surprising that some people to try to do this, because the society we live in supports that type of denial. But if there is any corner of your psyche that wishes to do such a thing, hopefully it will be called into serious conversation with your heart, so that your heart, mind, and soul can become attuned to the pathway to freedom.

What is the most profound challenge that you find being presented to you in this part of the book? Can you find a person with whom to speak about that challenge in honest ways who will help you to investigate it more deeply? What needs to happen to help you to move beyond the challenges discussed here? How can you and your community be helped by your work on the issues and ideas in this part?

Part 6

BROKENHEARTED

MEDITATION 31

The System Killed My Little Brother

My little brother died when he was twelve years old, and he took my father with him. Though my father passed many years later, it was merely a belated announcement of a much earlier death.

As people often did in rural areas, my family responded to my brother's physical complaints with home treatments until it became clear that he needed more than they were able to do. When he was taken to the local hospital, they refused to treat him because poor black people were not welcome there. The only alternative was the "charity hospital" for poor folks and people of color, which was located in Shreveport, Louisiana, about seventy miles from our family home. It took a few hours to arrange transportation and to travel there, and by the time he arrived he had gone into crisis. A ruptured appendix cost him his life.

My father never recovered from his inability to save my brother's life. He was brokenhearted for the remainder of his life, and he passed it to any of us who would join him. As a child I joined him in that brokenheartedness simply because he was my father and I adored him and wanted to be as close to him as possible. Today, I continue to live in that space in many ways because it informs my understanding of how the work of racial healing can be most effective.

If one does not stand in solidarity with those who suffer, becoming not just an observer but also a brokenhearted fellow pilgrim, it is so easy to step into the illusion of being the one who can fix someone or something, reinforcing the energy of superiority. This is a travesty, because that energy is part of what causes the suffering in the first place. Be the brokenhearted and you will see that the fixes are more complex.

Another opportunity to be brokenhearted came into my life when I was nearing the end of my college days. As a student at Pepperdine University in Los Angeles, I was provided a chance to stand up for justice in a way that I never had before the incident on our campus that left a young black male from the neighborhood dead in the spring of 1969.

The young man, Larry Kimmons, was killed by the campus security guard, a white man in his late seventies or early eighties who should not have been left with the task of providing security services for the campus in the rapidly changing environment of that time and the many challenges to the status quo that were occurring. Larry Kimmons came from a wonderful single-parent household, and his mother had visited with the security guard to make sure that it was appropriate for him to be on the campus to play basketball, as the neighborhood youngsters enjoyed doing. But on the Wednesday evening when he was shot to death at point-blank range by the guard, a new narrative was launched about him.

That evening the youngsters came to play basketball and were told that the gym was closed because it was Wednesday night and the campus was shut down for Bible study. They inquired about waiting for the gym to reopen after Bible study; though this had not been a problem before, somehow on this day it became a huge issue, and the security guard decided to run them off the campus. Larry was reported to have tried to reason with him and to remind him that his mother had come to speak to him about the teenagers being there. But the guard appeared to have forgotten about those conversations, or even that he knew the youngsters at all: he got his shotgun, aimed it at Larry, and shot him at close range. Larry died soon afterward.

Though this happened more than fifty years ago, the memory still lies in me at a cellular level. In fact, I have come to realize that much of my work is propelled by the desire to help make a world that does not need to feed off the blood of black children by refusing them medical care or shooting them down like snakes in the grass.

The events that followed this murder were devastating to all, and especially to black students. The administration did not want to send anyone to visit his mother, nor did they want to assist in paying for his funeral. We were already enraged, frightened, and brokenhearted, and the break in our hearts grew larger as over the next days and weeks we witnessed people who professed to be followers of Jesus act as if the young life that had been lost meant nothing. Some went a step further and tried to characterize him as a good-for-nothing, a menace, or a vagrant—as if any of those would be a reason to kill him. It soon became clear to me that we were not following the same Jesus.

The long struggle to force the university to act in a more humane, honorable manner toward Larry's family continues to be a part of many ongoing conversations today as some of us who are alumni work with the university to create an ongoing memorial to him. My cells will hold the memory, as long as I live, of Mrs. Clydie Kimmons's long, gut-wrenching scream at her young son's funeral. I pray never to forget that sound, because it helps me to remember that my work as an empowered, liberated person is to make sure that no one rests from the work of racial healing until all of the structures that support the notion that black life is expendable have been dismantled. It is a good reminder not to get lost in accommodating racism on any front and to spend each day trying to be open enough to the gift of courage to stay in solidarity with those who suffer on the margins. One potential trap we can fall into is that of becoming the "exceptional negro" or the "designated negro" or the only friend of color that a white person has managed to make. Allowing external forces such as this to shape our attitudes toward our siblings, whom racists deem worthy of continued oppression, makes it difficult to find true liberation. These forces themselves must be part of what we dismantle.

Being brokenhearted leads to clarity about our unwillingness to abide racist behavior. It is very disheartening to hear white people who are not trying to move beyond being allies try to explain acts of racist terror and other daily denigrations of people of color with oversimplifications instead of properly naming them. The energy generated from a broken heart will not engage with oversimplified ways of looking at the reality of what is happening in the lives of the oppressed as they strain under the weight of oppression and all the ways that it kills the body and injures the soul. It will not tolerate superficial answers to the real questions that must be answered by folks seeking to be liberated. Brokenheartedness is a prerequisite for truly becoming a fellow pilgrim and not simply an ally who can come and go from the resistance whenever it is convenient.

In many ways, brokenheartedness becomes a tool to assess the type of energy that whites are bringing to the racial healing conversation. There has to be a fair amount of pain associated with being a white person who is trying to be conscious but has to face the truth of how the American experiment has become a place where so much of people's identity is grounded in indefensible notions about the connection between skin color and human value. There is but one remedy for this, and it lies in learning to differentiate between yourself as an individual and the collective. While this is a big challenge, it can be done—and until it is done, immobilizing energies will run wild in the streets of your inner community. One of the most profound lessons that any of us can learn is to separate ourselves from the collective even as we work to see how we are related to it.

Part of the difficulty with working in white spaces is how hard it can be to step back from such spaces and look at the situation with a wider lens. The tiny lens of self-absorption that imagines everything, including racial issues, from the perspective of "What does it have to do with me and my well-being?" is too small and useless for anyone who is trying to be well. The white person who is trying to move along the path of overcoming personal racism will have to embrace the challenge of discerning what belongs in the category of personal concerns and what should be placed in the collective. Progressive whites have a fair amount of difficulty with this dynamic. The deep desire to be better than the rest when it comes to racism makes it difficult to name what needs to be named and to seek healing. The longer denial is engaged, the more comfortable it becomes to rest there, and the more difficult it is to move to new levels of awareness.

Clearly it is not any fun to experience a broken heart, but it is empowering to stay open to the process of engaging in suffering with others. If there is going to be any genuine, sustainable change toward racial healing, we must dismantle the constructs that restrict all who live in this land. When we allow our hearts to break for one another, a new dynamic of vulnerability can emerge that makes it possible to see in a new way. There are many points along the way when one can catch a glimpse of the new light of the morning, finally managing to outlive the darkness of the night. That light will be sustained by the continued willingness to walk in the shoes of another, especially those that are considered "other" among us.

MEDITATION 32

Can We Have a Word?
Victims Want to Be Heard

We were really just trying to live our lives. And we are wondering if we could ask you, a person who is white, a question. What part of the privilege that comes from having white skin are you willing to give up so that people in black and brown skin can just live, without the kind of violence that took our lives?

We realize that many of you are sad and very sorry that we were killed. Some of you are going out to march in the streets. Others are resorting to violence, which is unfortunate, because we do not think that will help the situation at all. Some of you are hosting vigils. You bring flowers to the places where we were murdered. You are outraged, as you should be. But, you see, we are gone, and we are not coming back.

Was there anything you could have done about the way you have chosen to travel through the world as a white person that could have helped to create a different world—a world where it would be inconceivable that a white person in a uniform could practice violence against folks in black and brown bodies without having to worry very much about the consequences for them?

How do you resist white supremacy? Is it only when a few of us get murdered in plain sight? How does white supremacy serve you? What parts of it are you ready to let go? What will that mean for you? What do you have to change? Are you willing and ready to make that change? We want to know. We have paid the ultimate price for the world that was made for you because for some reason we were sent into the world with black skin instead of white skin. So we think that we can ask you hard questions.

What part of your white skin privilege are you willing to give up so we can have a world that does not hate black and brown bodies so much? Once you know the answer to that question, please do it. And then light a candle for yourself in the hope that the light will grow larger and help you see what you need to do next.

Let our deaths not be in vain!

—George, Ahmaud, Breonna

In this moment, as we struggle with finding the path through our grief about losing too many young people to the racial terrorism perpetrated by white men, as in the case of Ahmaud Arbery, and by out-of-control law enforcement personnel, as in the cases of George Floyd and Breonna Taylor, we all have to pause. While white privilege certainly needs to be challenged in these cases, it is not enough. Often there is immediate, passionate response to the many deaths of young people of color at the hands of police and others, but it has not resulted in sustained work that creates the change that needs to come. Since the murder of George Floyd in 2020, hundreds of young black and brown people along with a handful of young whites have been killed under questionable circumstances by the police. And for the most part, we have barely paid enough attention to their deaths to even learn their names. We cannot afford to continue in this way.

Nor can we afford to give a platform to those voices that seek to minimize the situation by pointing out that young blacks and other people of color kill each other. Yes, it is true they do kill one another, and it is tragic. But using that fact in an attempt to justify unwarranted police killings and other uses of excessive force is an expression of racism doing its best to confuse the issues and avoid what is unavoidable.

We allow ourselves to become numbed to the pain of this issue because it seems as if there is no realistic path to a remedy. But that is an unacceptable response. Our broken hearts demand better of us, and we all have to decide whether we will say yes to the invitation to seek a better path.

Can you imagine what a better path might involve? It appears that the most essential element is for all of us to spend some time exploring what we really think about the lives of those other than ourselves and our immediate family and friends. Is all human life valuable? Does the Creator love everyone equally or not?? We have to take a stand on these things; there is no hiding out in some type of liminality. We have to figure out what we really believe.

It is true that there are many conversations about all of these questions, and many thoughtful folks are working very hard to imagine a new path forward. We have many miles to go before we arrive at a resting place, but it is good to be engaged in the conversation that is seeking remedies. Racism is at the core of this issue with policing. Our modern system of law enforcement has its historical roots in a system that grew out of the need to recapture folks during the era of slavery; thus race was always factored into this equation in the wrong manner. If we would take the energy we have spent on explaining away this problem and instead devote it to solving the problem, our communities would be far better off.

Many whites find it easy to lay responsibility for deaths such as Ahmaud Arbery's, George Floyd's, and Breonna Taylor's at the feet of blacks alone, many blacks find it easy to retreat into being ashamed and fearful. None of these responses are helpful; they do not change anything, and at the end of the day people of color are left to live in fear as the next person's life is taken.

Black shame and fear about this situation and white guilt and blame are such unhelpful expenditures of energy. While they may be briefly necessary as part of the clarifying process, they are not places to be occupied for the long run. How long will it take us to get to a better understanding, so that we can change the narrative and begin to reimagine the way forward? It would help all of us to begin a new type of reflection, one that might lead us to catch a glimpse of the morning light that longs to shine on this dangerous and frightening set of circumstances.

The voices of the many George Floyds, Ahmaud Arberys, and Breonna Taylors call to us to do better. We need to make sure that we step out of fear, shame, blame, and all the other things that immobilize us. We need to allow our hearts to be broken over and over until we arrive at the point of being willing to stand in the light that the morning wishes to bring.

MEDITATION 33

Reflection on Integration

The idea behind integration—that we needed to move from our separatist ways of the past to an environment where all spaces in this country are open to everyone—seems quite noble and necessary. But when we reflect upon what happened, what it cost, and who had to pay, we might wonder if we paid far too much for what we achieved through integration. It was supposed to be the big step toward genuine liberation for blacks and other people of color in America.

I have no trouble understanding what we thought we were going to achieve, but what integration in fact has achieved might be a very interesting question to sit with for a bit. Of course, we had to begin someplace; *Brown v. Board of Education* was a case that could be won, and it was wonderful to win it. But I have often wondered what we were thinking when we decided to send our little black children into hostile white environments to do the work that needed to be done by adults. Trying to break down the barriers of segregation was the right thing, but using the children was not the right choice about who should do the work.

Now that we know what we know about racialized trauma, it is startling to reflect upon the damage that was done to several generations of young people who as adults are still trying to navigate those injuries, which have never been acknowledged. Another troubling piece of this issue: while there were many physical and economic deficits in the educational resources for blacks compared to whites, there is no way to measure the psychological and spiritual resources that were lost in the effort to use school integration as a way to create a more just society.

It is also important to think about the injury to the black teachers who were forced to relocate to white environments as integration continued (though in the early years there were no black teachers in white schools). My family included several teachers, and one of them was my mother; I recall that when her small Arkansas school was integrated, all of the black teachers, including my mother, were fired. They brought a lawsuit against the school district, which they won. But my mother was recruited to a California school system, which proved to be quite challenging to her. I was in college at the time in California, but I did not talk to her very much about the nature of the difficulty; she would say a few things from time to time that made it clear she was navigating a difficult space.

All of this adds up to multiple layers of injuries that came out of integration and which contributed to the brokenhearted spaces that we have navigated for decades. We have not done any major work to acknowledge the depth of those injuries and brokenheartedness. But the loss that the black community experienced around moving away from schools that were safe havens for students and teachers deserves to be taken into careful consideration. When that loss is factored in, there is far too little net gain. Furthermore, when we reflect upon the present moment, we see major polarization in education across the country.

Unfortunately, it takes more than putting together people who represent different groups to achieve diverse, healthy, functioning, sustainable communities, and that factor seemed to have been left out of the equation as integration was being embraced. People need to come together with the intention to create such spaces. But when that is left to happenstance, the outcomes generally have not been the most positive, as we have witnessed around the efforts of desegregation. It might be a wonderful project for a group of thoughtful people to come together and work on designing an intentional community that reflects true diversity.

There is reason to believe that our religious communities could be a catalyst for creating such spaces, but we know what a failure most of them have been in terms of creating spaces where there is an honest and deep sharing of life journeys with racial healing as a central focus. Most of the white religious communities that were so focused on Jesus during periods of racial awakening in the 1960s and 1970s were trying to make sure that their members bought their declaration that everything was fine because Jesus was being appropriated in great new ways and because skin color did not matter. As I write this today, I am grateful that I never believed most of that narrative, which I heard in white house churches during my college years. It did not ring true to my soul, and I resisted it. There were times when some of the members of those groups were very unhappy with me because I continued to seek paths of racial and political liberation.

Separatism is not an answer to racism; let me be clear about that. But neither is forcing folks to occupy space together when there is no intention to have such groups make sense to the folks who have to live the reality of them on a daily basis. And it is clear to me that children should never be the ones who have to carry this burden. If they are included as a part of their family systems, that is a different issue, but to send a lone child into spaces that are less than welcoming is cruel and should not be done for any reason.

What are your thoughts about integration? Is your community racially diverse or not? How does this meditation engage you as you reflect upon the thoughts shared in it? Can you find someone who cares about these matters and speak to them about it also?

Proximity is essential, but it should be engaged with a great sense of consciousness and care for everyone who is involved in it. We have to stay deeply grounded in the truth that whether one is white, black, or brown, good soul-keeping work must accompany the deep work of developing consciousness and opening up the journey to racial healing in new ways.

MEDITATION 34

Killing Fields

If you are a white, black, or brown person who wonders why we should be so concerned about police killing our children when they seem to be so committed to killing one another, it might be helpful to sit for a bit with some of the complicated threads that have been woven into the fabric of many of our communities of color. In the ones that are experiencing extreme poverty, the lack of resources such as grocery stores, recreational facilities, health-care, decent educational opportunities, a healthy environment, safe housing, and many other sources of negative energy makes it difficult to believe that there is any light to come in the morning. When we find it acceptable to force people to spend every waking moment trying to determine how to survive from day to day with far less resources than they actually need, violence against self and others is the result.

The way in which we have organized our society has accomplished what it was intended to do: blacks, other people of color, and poor people have historically been disenfranchised and are treated in an ongoing way as if they are second-class citizens. The drawing of lines between the poor and the rich, and between people of color and whites, was not accidental: those lines were deliberately and carefully drawn and maintained. Thus it is not surprising that many of the spaces those lines created are now spiraling downward into violence and what seems to be an endless list of unsolvable problems.

The truth is that those places can and would do better if we began paying attention to them and making efforts to help them emerge from their long struggles. But we are not trying to do that, because those spaces are succeeding at keeping those folks contained in their respective places. Here's an example from my own experience. In 1997, the president of Mercer University, where I worked as an assistant professor and director of African American studies, granted me the honor of working for the mayor of Macon, Georgia, for two years as a loaned executive. I served as the director of the mayor's Youth Violence Prevention Task Force during that time, and it was the hardest work that I have ever done in my life. I wept myself to sleep more during those two years than I did when I was doing an internship on the oncology unit at Grady Hospital as part of my work toward a master's in social work.

The summer I began that work, we had more than thirty young people murdered in Macon, a city with fewer than 160,000 people. There was serious gang activity in the city, and while we were engaging with a Weed and Seed project (this was during the Clinton administration), it was going to take much more than a few AmeriCorps volunteers on bicycles in those troubled neighborhoods and a few computers in a nicely painted new building to impact the activity on the killing fields. The unmanaged rage that was born out of a sense of hopelessness and helplessness was palpable whenever I met with young folks from some of our neighborhoods.

One of the programs that we did during that time was to organize youngsters to paint murals in areas that had been heavily impacted by gang graffiti. That work was and continues to be amazingly positive, because the gangs did not mar the murals. It seemed like a miracle at the time, and much to my surprise, those murals are still intact, though that work was done several decades ago.

In addition to painting murals, we raised money and bought back guns from the youngsters. Thankfully, we had a very progressive police chief who believed that every gun we bought back was one less gun on the streets, and his support was important in making that effort successful. Though it was years ago, I can still hear many of those very young, mostly black males voicing their fear of being on the streets without a gun. Some who showed up at those Saturday gun buybacks looked as if they were twelve or thirteen years old. They were babies, yet already living under the illusion that a gun would make them safe.

Of course, the message that guns are necessary is still being sent across the land, as it has been for a very long time. What a lie this is, and how dangerous for a child to believe that the way ahead for his young life is to be able to kill people before they kill him. Many of these youngsters did not believe for a second that they would live to be eighteen years old or that they would graduate from high school. What heartbreaking words came from their young mouths—and, unfortunately, how true they were.

During my time there, a group called Mourning Mothers made a quilt to memorialize all the young people who had been murdered (the group included women and a few men who had lost their children to violence, but only the women worked on the quilt once that project was started). The project was led by a fabric artist who helped to direct the work. Each person created a panel of remembrance for their lost son or daughter. They brought in things that reminded them of the murdered person, along with a photograph that was silkscreened onto fabric that would become part of the quilt. It was an amazing project. We cried a lot. The parents supported one another. There were times when someone simply couldn't take it anymore and would throw her things in the trash, proclaiming that she was not coming back. Someone else would get her things out of the trash and put them away till the next meeting, when that person would return and be glad that her things had not been destroyed. Once the quilt was finished it was placed in City Hall for a portion of its life, and then it was moved to the Macon Convention Center. The quilt was finally taken down, and I have no idea what happened to it. But after I left and the mayor for whom I worked left, others thought it was too gruesome and did not want to have to look at it. That in itself was part of the problem. After all, these were our children who had died, and yet as a community we could not stand to remember them.

All the efforts we made during that period were superficial, because we were not really doing anything to destabilize the racist structure that supported the neglect of the neighborhoods where much of the killing was taking place. There were meetings, promises of help, proclamations, studies, little pots of money, youth entrepreneurship programs designed to divert middle-school students from the pathway to joining a gang, and numerous other notions about solutions to the violence and the guns. But youngsters were still scared and still did not feel safe in their homes. Worse, their neighborhoods were the target of constant surveillance by police and others who were interested only in confirming what they thought they already knew about these neighborhoods—which was that there was no point in bothering with them because they were too far gone.

Children cannot thrive when people have given up on them. Though a few of these youngsters did survive, far too many of them ended up dead before reaching the age of eighteen, and many others went to prison through the school-to-prison pipeline. The young person in the street with his gun desires to do something to make life better and wishes to be safe, but he has no way of knowing that the racist culture has relegated him to a path leading him to the prison bed that has been imagined for him or to the cemetery.

As I said, I cried more during that time than I did when I was working with folks dying of cancer, because I felt helpless at times, simply trying to think of ways to engage these young people who could not believe that there was any reason for them to have hope. We persevered. We worked with them making pillows and jewelry to sell on Saturday mornings. We kept painting murals. We talked. We bought back guns. We talked some more. Some were saved. Too many were lost. Our hearts were broken, and they continue to be broken. We dare not blame them for killing one another when death is the only thing that makes perfect sense to them.

I believe that we can make a better world than this for the young folks who continue to populate our cities. Even if we don't do it well, we owe it to them to try. Come and bring your broken heart. Join us.

MEDITATION 35

Broken Hearts Cure Illusion

It is very challenging to stay focused as we explore racism, because there are so many illusions associated with this system. A central one, of course, is that some humans are better than others. One way this has played out is through whites struggling with the privilege of having white skin. Of course, that is a constructed privilege, and it has been lived into in ways that often make it seem defensible—that is part of the illusion. A socialization process reinforcing the belief that some people are superior because their skin happens to not be black or brown is fraught with a deep sense of untruth, but if people are fed that idea beginning early in life, they will have great difficulty letting it go.

White people have internalized the narrative of white skin privilege, and that makes it quite difficult to see its fallacy. In addition, it offers a framework that shapes the path of life in ways that provide comfort and security. Those benefits are very difficult to relinquish, of course. Realizing this makes it easier to understand why white people find it so difficult to vacate the idea of white privilege. On the other hand, those who have not had the privilege of being taught that the world is theirs find this position very hard to imagine.

While young black and brown people today have a better chance than earlier generations did of beginning to imagine that the world is theirs too, they still find it very difficult to navigate the oppressive systems that are structured to keep black and brown folks away from privilege. The truth is that everyone deserves to have the best life possible, and it is the Creator's intention that it should be so. But the cultural patterns that support racial stratification have no intention of supporting the view that black or brown skin is equal to white skin. The racist narrative cannot abide that notion.

Therefore, black and brown youngsters need to be taught to have a sense of self that is not predicated upon being outer-directed, as they cannot expect a culture that is not yet interested in seeing them as equals to afford them the entitlement that they believe belongs to them. While they may have a sense of being free as long as they don't challenge too many of racism's mandated controls, that is an illusion of equality. Teaching them their history will help them to gain a clearer understanding of reality.

Suffering is also a good teacher, and it helps those who engage it to see a bit deeper than the ones who work to avoid it at all costs. Someone who listens and learns from the grief of being brokenhearted can see through illusions better than the person who refuses to go on that path. At some point along the way, a white person will come up against a challenge to the notion that whiteness equals superiority. This can be painful if the illusion has been held as fact for a lifetime, as is the case for many whites. While suffering is never to be glorified, it is good to welcome it in a case such as this, because it will lead to a path where illusion is continuously challenged, and that challenge is necessary for consciousness to have a chance to flourish.

Of course, suffering in and of itself does not necessarily result in anything except seeking to find new ways to resist; for it to teach us something, we must open our hearts to it. When it comes to privilege, a fair amount of intentionality is required to relinquish any of it. I recall standing in a room with a white man who was enraged by my conversation challenging his privilege, and he finally said what was really the absolute truth for him: "What's wrong with it and why would I want to give it up?" That question is not unusual. But it deserves to be investigated carefully if we have made a commitment to living in the world in a life-supporting way. If we are mostly interested in holding on to our privilege and living within all of the structures that make life work well for us, then why should we have any interest in letting go of privilege? But if another path seems to make any sense, and if we have an inkling that there is more to living in the world than simply getting our wishes fulfilled, then there will be a tiny opening for things to be different.

The inner and outer conflicts will present themselves often and loudly when the journey toward consciousness begins, and the heart that is open to being broken will be able to see more clearly where the truth can be found. Each day brings many invitations to engage. What are the invitations being offered to you? What do they appear to be offering you in exchange for the status quo? What will it take to explore them? Do they seem filled with energy that is inviting or with energy that is condemning?

The Gift of Being Brokenhearted

If we are strong enough to be weak enough, we are given a
wound that never heals. It is the gift that keeps the heart open.

—Oriah, *The Invitation*

It is hard to face pain, whether emotional or physical. But life will
not be fully lived until we come to terms with suffering, which is
an inescapable fact of life on the planet. The effort to escape suffering has led us to this very strange place of seeking to stay numb
enough not to notice the suffering. Addictions, violence, runaway
materialism, fundamentalist thinking, religion that wants to make
God a personal errand runner, and many other extremes are employed in the effort to avoid pain.

The public watched with horror as Russia invaded Ukraine in
2022, much as we have watched many other great tragedies in the
world. The pain and sorrow caused by acts of inhumanity and bar-
barism call forth a multiplicity of emotions. But at the end of the
day we are left with nothing but our sorrow and frustration. While
our leaders seem to be able to do virtually whatever they want, each
of us, as one individual, is quite limited; even when we give money
to aid organizations, it is no consolation. What are we left to do?

Some people are tempted to justify the suffering, as I have oc-
casionally heard from some in response to this invasion. Others
try to forget that it is happening by refusing to engage it in any
manner. The problem with responses intended to avoid the pain

is that they do not come without a cost. Each time a person chooses a path of avoidance, small parts of their life shrink. Their heart becomes more closed, and new possibilities to live fully become compromised.

The Russian invasion of Ukraine loomed large in front of us, but there are innumerable other instances when avoidance was the method employed to address painful situations instead of taking the time to engage with them and accepting whatever outcomes resulted. We see this regarding race in America as more white people search for ways to minimize the pain of history. I have spoken in these meditations about many painful threads that are woven into the fabric of life in America and especially about how some of those dynamics play out regarding relationships between black and white women. The previous meditations in this part have addressed several very profound sources of brokenheartedness that seem almost impossible to navigate. Sadly, there is a huge temptation to avoid the entire subject if possible, or to minimize it, or do anything with the ideas except engage them.

To use Oriah's words, if we ever become strong enough to be weak enough to accept the wound that comes to live in our heart when we say yes to the invitation to be brokenhearted as we walk through this life, we will be freer. The effort to avoid the pain causes folks to argue about the validity of history or to simply try to ban things such as the 1619 Project. Honestly, it is very sad to think that a thoughtful adult would believe that simply saying "We don't want to know about the history because we do not want to be upset" will take them to a safe place where there will be no pain related to race. There is no such corner on this earth; racism has been exported around the world. Denial of history is not a remedy.

Whether it is the Russian invasion of Ukraine, systemic racism, or a friend dying, the only remedy that works is sitting quietly and having one's heart opened by pain, which creates the space to hold the pain. This acceptance will lead to the birth of new possibilities for living everyday life better and for opening new areas that were completely unknown. Denial helps to keep this access to a larger life hidden.

When we are in the middle of pain, it is very difficult to see that it has any purpose except to cause destabilization and misery, but efforts to avoid pain simply create more misery in the long run. One expression of that misery is fear, which comes from the realization that pain can never truly be avoided. Rather than try futilely to erase the fear, remember that the world is eagerly awaiting those with the courage to be brokenhearted. Take a brave half step in that direction and see how it serves you.

Part 7

THE OUTER WORLD NEEDS YOU

MEDITATION 37

Let Me Tell a Story That I Like

While we can tell any story that we like, when it comes to history, it is a good idea to tell the truth. The movement across the land, especially in the Southeast, to rewrite American history to suit the images that unconscious white people wish to see is quite disturbing. It is difficult to believe that people who appear to be adults and have major political and social responsibility in our world are able to put forth pieces of legislation intended to make sure that their children are not disturbed by their education.

If one could manage to live a lifetime without being disturbed, that would be both remarkable and a strange event indeed. It does not take much reflection to come to the realization that there is an inextricable relationship between being disturbed and becoming the person that one was put upon the earth to be. In the world of Jungian psychology, that work is called individuation. It is the process of growing into being your own person instead of being the same as everyone else on the planet. Growing and becoming, dying and being reborn, opening to new possibilities while old ones go away—all around us is affirmation of this process, and it causes plenty of disturbance. So it is ludicrous to assume that one can escape the turmoil of living in the world, though there are many who work quite diligently to keep this illusion intact. "Let me tell the story that I like instead of the truth even as I see it," they say. But it is dangerous to live in a world constructed on the premise that any lie will do if it helps to avoid pain.

Whether we are reflecting upon personal history or that of our community, church, social club, or any other entity with a history, whatever happened is the truth that we have to tell. To do anything other than exercise as much integrity as possible in the telling of that story is not helpful and is more likely to cause more harm in the future than the pain of the truth will cause in the present moment. In the United States the historical record is not a pleasant one, and in some cases it is absolutely horrible, but it is our history. It is a history shared by all who live here; we do not have to like it, but we do have to accept that it is what we have. It is sad that there are people among us who wish to simply take what they like and leave the rest and believe that it is their right and responsibility to tell others which parts they can take and which they must leave.

This attitude reflects one of the deep wounds that racism has left on such people, which is the illusion of superiority and control and a sense of empowerment that is dangerous in a free society. One person does not get the opportunity to control what can be taught, learned, and heard in a free society; those who think that way will cause the rest of society to have to stand against them at some point, and if that energy gets played out to its fullest extent, it can lead to war. While I tend to stay away from being an alarmist, I do believe that there are people out there, those who commit to lies and make up their ethical positions as they go, who would enjoy seeing us in a civil war. There is already enough war in their inner communities, and pairing that with their commitment to unconsciousness can be powerful enough to fuel the fires of negative energy that would manifest as violence and war if given any small chance.

Since it appears that this type of energy is traveling quite comfortably across America at the moment, it is more critical than ever to make sure that those who are trying to remain open to the truth and be a half shade braver each day stay focused and take every possible step to disrupt this negative energy by proclaiming the good news of healing and hope. This does not mean that everyone has to embrace a cheerleading-type energy and turn somersaults in the grass, but it does mean soberly acknowledging the reality that every word, thought, and action matters in the grand scheme of healing and wellness. It matters what we think and how we think it. It matters what we say and how we say it. It matters whether we seek to be loving or settle for merely appearing to be loving.

Authenticity matters, and everyone with any sense of how much that matters to walking the path toward consciousness will seek to be as authentic as possible. Perhaps you are wondering how it will help. It will help because the truth matters. Everyone who lives more than five years on the earth knows that people will lie. But it is quite problematic when we have adults who are willing to stand in front of a microphone and declare that there is something called "alternative facts" as a way to justify their lies. Where there is any interest in creating spaces where people can be well and live their lives to the fullest, there has to be a handful of agreed-upon truths that folks accept as a part of the fabric that helps to reinforce trust. And there has to be respect for the life and humanity of all who are a part of the group.

As you engage with all the various challenges that will show up in your inner community and outer world, it is crucial to stand up and tell the best truth possible. Stand against the "any lie will do" mentality and the willingness to sacrifice the truth for a good season of trending on Twitter or some other social media platform. The outer world needs you to tell the story as it is to the best of your knowledge.

MEDITATION 38

Quit Worrying about Critical Race Theory

Today is a good day to quit worrying about critical race theory and to decide to help silence the massive amount of negative chatter surrounding it. The furor around critical race theory is a profound example of making up the story that you want to tell instead of telling the story that happens to be true; in this case it is done for the purpose of fueling the negative fires of racism and deceit, and it is far too successful. Our limited energy can be spent in debates far better than this one.

Contrary to what the disinformation machine blares, critical race theory (CRT) is not a body of scholarship that is on its way to the local public school (or college, for that matter). Your child's elementary or high school teacher will not be sending them home with books on it. Clearly, many of the loudest people proclaiming its dangers have no idea what actually constitutes CRT, nor do they know how it originated. We can see this by the manner in which they speak about it as if every elementary and high school student is about to be inundated with this weird thing called CRT.

We should all take a deep breath and pay a bit of attention to what CRT is and how it came into being in the first place. Perhaps having this bit of background can be very helpful the next time there is a conversation on this topic with folks who are not sure what they are speaking about but are gripped by fear of it. At the beginning the field was called critical legal studies, and it started with a group of legal scholars (who included the late Derrick Bell,

Kimberlé Crenshaw, Cheryl Harris, Richard Delgado, Patricia Williams, Gloria Ladson-Billings, Tara Yosso, and others) who were working to find the best ways to approach racial justice work. They found a great fallacy in the argument that the law is objective, neutral, principled, and not influenced by social and political considerations. They believed that the law could be complicit in helping to maintain an unjust social order by reproducing racial inequality.

Their inquiry led them to the formulation of CRT, which consists of "a body of legal scholarship and an academic movement of civil rights scholars and activists in the United States that seek to critically examine U.S. law as it intersects with issues of race in the U.S. and to challenge mainstream American liberal approaches to racial justice."[21] It has to be quite clear that this body of legal scholarship is not about to replace the curriculum of any local public or private K-12 school or college in any manner, and no one who is talking about it believes that it will unless they do not understand what it is.

The following are some of the foundational questions that this group of scholars raised regarding the law: How does the law construct race? How has the law protected racism and upheld racial hierarchies? How does the law reproduce racial inequality? These continue to be very good questions for all of us to ponder, and especially those who are in the legal world working to foster justice. The group studying these issues went on to ask: How can the law be used to dismantle race, racism, and racial inequality? They asked this question because they believed it was very difficult for the law to serve as the major dismantling force of racism since it was often used to reinforce it.

Major examples of this type of complicity between the law and racism are found in such instances as the failure of the Supreme Court to outline a specific remedy to end segregated education in the *Brown* case, or assuming that the Fourteenth Amendment alone could promote racial equality for black people when this remedy was a threat to the superior social status of white people. Though the law can be used to support racial equality, it is imperative that such laws be carefully crafted and that there is the political will to enforce them once they are in place.

The major point of this discussion is to help put CRT back where it belongs, in the arena of legal scholarship, instead of holding it up as something that parents of small children should fear. To reiterate, no young person from kindergarten through grade 12 will hear their teacher giving a lesson on critical race theory. However, teaching children about racism and its impact upon all of us is a completely different issue.

All the nonsense that has built up around CRT stems from the imagination of a few racists who needed to give their racism a press agent. Please, stand against this behavior and help to imagine a new world where the truth is more important than fiction. Don't allow this conversation to be conducted in your presence as if it deserves legitimate concern.

Racism and its impact fuel the disinformation campaign about CRT. By raising such a firestorm of misinformation, this effort hopes to draw attention away from the real issue of racial injustice and inequality, which is hurting us all. It is essential that all thoughtful folks help put an end to this conversation and not allow it to continue to spread.

MEDITATION 39

The Media Need to Stop Being Racism's Press Agent

It is clear that all forms of media can be either helpful or harmful when it comes to the dissemination of information. But it is equally clear that many of those in the media do not seem to understand that themselves—or perhaps they are just driven by profit motives that impact their behavior. While it is difficult to answer the question of why they behave as they do, it is simple to reflect upon their behavior and the ways in which it has an impact upon us.

This is a bit challenging to explore, so I want to use the CRT discussion that was highlighted in the previous meditation as a backdrop. The media helped to create the firestorm around CRT. It does not take very long to research the roots of CRT and understand quite clearly what its purpose was and continues to be. But instead of presenting this information in a clear-headed and honest way that could have helped the public know what this entire conversation was really about, the media in all markets kept playing to the false narrative generated by racists. This is a serious matter. All who care about the truth, no matter what color your skin happens to be, should be chagrined to the point of disgust about how this has been handled. That false narrative should have been stopped before it got the type of tailwind that caused it to spread like wildfire.

Please don't be confused here. This is not an argument about censorship or free speech. This is about integrity and a commitment to truth. Every day there are stories that are not reported, for any number of reasons—and not always noble ones. While I do not work in that world on a regular basis, I have some experience with the media industry. It is controlled by humans who bring their strengths and weakness to the equation, as is the case in any profession. But when one is dealing with the building or destruction of public trust, it pays to tread with great care and caution. The hype around CRT is one very good, easily discernible example of the larger issue confronting us as a people as we try to crawl our way to a more balanced place when it comes to racial polarization and the future of our lives together on the planet.

Racism does not deserve a press agent, and the country does not need it to have one. Media outlets could make a very large and grand contribution to healing the soul of this country and the world if they could find the courage to be more concerned about the truth and its impact upon the quality of life for everyone rather than whatever appears to get them more views. While some of those in the industry do appear to be interested in doing more than simply beating the competition, their voices need support from the general public and others in their business. We can do better.

For instance, a public forum could have been hosted by any of the media outlets to expose the issue underlying the CRT controversy; it would have been a great opportunity to make the story about setting the record straight and respecting the truth. This is true, of course, for all who are able to speak, think, and write. Around any issue there is an opportunity to craft a response that can defuse inflammatory rhetoric, counter disinformation, and head off other efforts to injure instead of heal.

In the racial healing work I am engaged in, I hear many questions about what to do to advance the work. Sometimes it is simply a matter of being unwilling to take part in this type of inflammatory process, whether by being silent, by encouraging others to really think about what they are saying, or by taking an active stand to stop the process altogether. It is easy to fall into immobilization. We might wonder if we are violating some unspoken rule or, even worse, that a friend or family member might be offended by what is being said. But it is important to weigh whether that type of concern should be the deciding factor given what is at stake in our land. In another meditation, I commented that I believe there are those who would be glad to see our nation move into a civil war. Whether that is totally accurate or not, it is difficult to think that anyone reading this book would not be concerned by the level of energy around polarization today.

Dr. Martin Luther King Jr. wondered decades ago if we were heading for chaos or community. It seems clear that we need to continue to ask that question of ourselves. But the more important question might be which one we want—chaos or community? There are far too many indications that chaos suits us better than community. This is especially true if we think about the lack of civility, the fear-production machinery that is operating on too many fronts (particularly in the world of conspiracy theories), and the general commitment to lying even though the truth is standing in plain sight wishing to be acknowledged.

Going back to the question about what to do to advance the work of racial healing, I will say that one of the easiest yet simultaneously most challenging places to occupy is the space of being committed to truth-telling regardless of where it leads. Racism's greatest enemy is the truth. But it does not have to worry too much, because there is so much willingness in so many circles to search for ways to avoid the truth or to make it less troubling. Thus, when you ask yourself, "What can I do?" the first answer is to commit to telling the best truth that you can find and to do so without apology. When this becomes a way of being for more of us, more sustainable change for the better will be the result. While it might be psychologically costly, truth-telling will not affect your checkbook—unless you have a job in the outer world that is more interested in appearances than the truth, and if that is the case, you might wish to find a new job.

Fortunately, there are times when such courageous acts can lead to new life. There is always enough power to act if we have enough courage to take the first step.

Racism does not need media outlets to help it. It does not deserve a press agent. But if the media do not see their way clear to charting a path like the one described in these pages, individuals can act. We can take a stand that exemplifies a truth-seeking and truth-telling way through the world. The first step is to make the deep inner commitment and then to pay attention to the ways in which it can be lived out in the larger community. This particular issue demonstrates the lovely rhythm between inner and outer work: as each person who finds the courage and capacity to act accordingly steps onto the path, the outcomes will help to create positive energy in the outer world.

MEDITATION 40

Colorism and Ubuntu

The idea that skin color is identity has its roots in color consciousness, which is the unnatural assignment of mental or moral traits
(negative or positive) based upon physical skin color. For example,
some believed that the African's black skin was considered evidence
that he was destined to serve as a slave.[22] Masters and overseers engaging in sex with female captives led after some time to a group of
mixed-race persons called mulattoes, whose hair and skin looked
more like the slavemaster's. But as time passed there was concern
among enslavers that mulattoes would band together against their
plight. Thus the "one-drop rule" was instituted, which declared
that one was African if there was one drop of African blood in
them.

While there were many ways in which the phenomenon of
colorism could have evolved, it has become a source of negativity
across the world. It has worked against the understanding that "I
am because we are," or Ubuntu, a powerful notion of our oneness
as humans on the planet. Despite the possibility that Ubuntu
could have been a catalyst for fostering unity in the slave community and communities of Africans as they were dispersed over
the globe, the master narrative proclaiming white skin superiority
instead helped create a sense of "otherness" among people who
were the same in terms of skin color, race, and who were enslaved
but began to labor under the illusion of difference because some
looked more like the master. The chance to stand together in

solidarity was short-circuited by the negative narratives wielded against the darker-skinned Africans along with a few small concessions to those with lighter skin, which made it appear that the skin difference was far more important than it really was. This helped to create the spaces that continue to this day where skin color and hair texture are seen as positive and negative traits.

This issue is not limited to the United States, but it is deeply ingrained in the fabric of black life in America. Listen to these words Big Bill Broonzy sang sixty years ago about America's Jim Crow system: "If you is white, you's all right, if you's brown, stick around, but if you's black, hmm, hmm, brother, get back, get back, get back."[23] There are many circles where the darker-skinned black person hears the message to get back. This is true despite the "black is beautiful" campaign of the 1960s and the many later attempts to hold up darker skin as being equal in value to skin that's lighter and mixed with white. The issue of colorism is quite a challenge. In the first place, those whose skin is darker have to develop a sense of self that does not allow this way of thinking to rule. The effort to do that is challenged by voices in the community that reinforce the notion of lighter skin as superior; often the voices might be in one's own family. This notion was spoken about in my family in rather subtle ways, mostly around the colors of clothing that should be chosen or avoided. The bright colors, especially red, that I happen to like best of all were discouraged. While I listened to these suggestions in my younger years, I have come to be a person who wears all of the colors that I enjoy, including red—and as much of it at one time as possible. It is a part of my declaration of personhood and my understanding that my worth is not determined by my skin tone or by my choice of colors.

However, I must confess that when a black woman professional colleague said to me, "You should make sure to marry a white man so your children will not be too dark, because you are so dark," it took me a few minutes to recover my breath. That comment was disturbing on many levels, and one of the most obvious questions it raised for me was what this woman, who was closer to what we call brown than black, thought of her very dark and stunningly handsome husband and of her beautiful daughter, who had her father's great skin color and beauty. The absurdity of that conversation is paralleled only by the sadness that it creates even to this day as I remember it and write these words. There are far too many blacks in this country and elsewhere laboring under this negative weight and far too many of them helping to keep the skin bleaching cream business going. Far too many of them feel bad about themselves and find it difficult to reach past those negative narratives about skin color to form strong ties with those who look like them. There is much healing work yet to be done around this issue.

One can observe how colorism manifests by paying attention to blacks working in certain professions, especially media and those who are used in advertising campaigns. A few of the folks will be darker, but most often anchors and others with public-facing positions will be as light as possible and have many features that might be associated with white skin. Hair texture accompanies this dilemma and simply complicates it.

There are black circles where racialized trauma has not been acknowledged and where whiteness is preferred and exclusion practiced on the basis of skin color. Of course, it is rarely, if ever, dealt with in a straightforward manner, but until it is, there will be no complete healing available to members of communities where these attitudes prevail.

The best example of liberation is exemplified by the black person who has genuinely confronted this issue and is able to live in the joy of being the person created by the Creator and has been given an opportunity to live in the beauty and wonder of being a part of that Creator. Embracing this fact makes it possible to celebrate life as the light rises in the morning and makes it clear that skin color has nothing to do with saying "good morning" each day in a deep and abiding sense of solidarity with the Creator and all of life.

Disappeared Communities: Where Are They Now?

Across our amazing country we have committed a set of deeply troubling acts by displacing communities in the name of progress without much thought. Many of those communities were made up of people of color who were very often not allowed to live in any spaces except those designated for blacks. They accepted those restrictions and went about the business of making lives for themselves and their families. For the most part it did not occur to them that they would ever have to face the devastation of being displaced, dispersed, and disappeared as if they never existed and did not matter. We called it progress. We called it urban renewal. We called it gentrification. They called it loss.

On many levels it matters not what outsiders called it; it was devastating, destabilizing, traumatizing, and injurious to those who were being forced to relocate. In some cases, the communities were totally destroyed: a once-thriving black community in Georgia is now a fine lake, and another is a large mall. And no one seems to mind that lives were turned upside down. We build roads across and through those communities, or we put in bus lines, all in the name of a greater good. But it is not quite good enough to simply note that this happened without asking what price was paid for this so-called progress and who paid it.

In all cases those areas were known as "home" to those who lived there. Designations such as "expendable," "ghetto," "blighted," and so on came from developers and others with agendas that had nothing to do with the welfare of the folks who were going to suffer the most. But those designations prevailed because of the power imbalance and the racist structures that supported them.

Who lived in those communities? Where did they have to go?? And one additional question: Who cares? Well, in answer to "Who cares?" one could say everyone who has any interest in collective wellness. Even though we have allowed ourselves to forget what "I am because we are," Ubuntu, means in our daily interactions with one another, the principle of needing to care about the collective community and the positive energy it generates matters. The Ubuntu idea matters when we try to create healing energy in our communities.

Can you begin to imagine with me the amount of grief that has been caused by taking homes from people, destroying their community, disrupting support systems for children and the elderly, forcing them to become scattered and separated? When the Department of Housing and Urban Development instituted its HOPE VI program in 1992, there was massive displacement of families because many of those who lived in the old housing stock that was being replaced could not afford to return, but at least HOPE VI pretended that it was attempting to improve living arrangements for the former public housing residents. The programs that built malls or highways didn't even pretend to offer folks anything.

I caught a glimpse of something important while listening to a colleague at the Absalom Jones Episcopal Center for Racial Healing share her interest in identifying the disappeared black communities in Atlanta, though it took several conversations with her before it dawned on me that she was onto something crucial. Finally I asked if she would be interested in putting together a resource guide listing the disappeared communities and providing a bit of information about them. She was delighted to do so. It occurred to me that it would be wonderful to identify folks who had lived in those communities and record their stories, which could be made available on the Center's website. Along with this we could partner with the City of Atlanta, the Visitors Bureau, and appropriate others to place markers at all of the sites, develop a brochure describing them, and invite folks who come to Atlanta to visit the sites and to listen to the stories of those who once lived in these spaces, which were made sacred by the precious lives that inhabited them.

The oral histories will be recorded in a series of small storytelling sessions, with two to four residents of the former communities brought together along with a small intergenerational audience. Afterward the sessions will be edited and placed on the website. We anticipate that people's long-held grief around the loss of their former lives will be abated a bit by this opportunity to engage in a form of public lament and to have their grief and loss acknowledged.

We are choosing this way to show up in the outer community and sharing it here to invite others to do the same if there seems to be any energy in the idea for them. The practice of city leaders making decisions about what constitutes progress and making decisions that benefit some folks while harming others is one to be rigorously interrogated.

This type of work might help to shine a bit of light upon processes that we so readily engage in without considering the consequences for people's lives. It is important to seek new paths that do not require such inequitable suffering. It is exciting to wonder how we might move forward with city planning and supporting communities of color instead of creating a dynamic in which there is no way to avoid the destruction. The truth is that we do know better. We do not make such choices for communities that are deemed worthy of being preserved. We spend a lot of money in Atlanta and many other major cities preserving historic areas and entities. So what is the underlying issue when it comes to communities of color? Unfortunately, it is not much of a mystery. They are seen as "less than" compared to many other communities, and no one in power thinks it's a problem to simply take them over. After all, who is going to stop it? There is racism again, standing in front of us, waving its hands, and making it clear that it is holding on to the place that belongs to it.

But that energy can be interrupted. It does not have to continue simply because it has been able to have its way for so long. All people, white, black, and brown, can join their voices to speak for a new way to engage in imagining our cities. Can we begin to consider that we might plan our cities in a way that affirms the humanity of everyone and the value of all life, no matter which neighborhood we happen to be speaking about? What will it require to change the narrative? It is our intention to use this project on disappeared communities to begin to create a new narrative, and to see if enough energy can be generated around it to globalize it.

Have you thought much about the places that no longer are habitable or that have been erased by progress in your city? Do you know where they were located? What about the displaced residents, what were their stories, their hopes, their fears? How did they feel about what happened? How might all of the change have been done in a different manner if those who were being displaced had been involved in conversations with those imagining the change? How would it have been different if they had been seen as equals, deserving to have a voice?

MEDITATION 42

Reclaiming Hope through Remembering

On October 22, 2016, the Episcopal Diocese of Atlanta took a bold step forward to begin a three-year cycle of pilgrimages to Georgia sites of martyrdom, most commonly known as lynching sites. The Beloved Community: Commission for Dismantling Racism (which became the Absalom Jones Center in 2017) believed that those sites needed to be viewed as places where martyrs were made. And all of us, whites and people of color, who make up the generations of their descendants needed to acknowledge them as martyrs and mark the places where their lives were sacrificed, in the hope that dawn would break on a future day when this legacy of terror could be vanished forever.

This chance for the birth of new hope was made viable through an honest declaration of what the past had been and why it was that way. We knew that the wounds of the past would not disappear simply because we wished for that to be the case. The work of healing had to be done. And we believed that each time we looked at the facts of history, without trying to make them more acceptable so we would not have to feel the pain of guilt, we took a step forward in the direction of healing. Our quest for hope in the twenty-first century required us to look back at this legacy before we could take the much-needed steps that would lead us forward.

During the time between the Civil War and World War II, thousands of African Americans were lynched in our country. This was the method used to terrorize African Americans into submission.

The victims were men, women, and children. Lynchings were intended to create racial subordination, quell resistance, and instill a fear-based atmosphere in which racial inequality could thrive. This inequality has yet to be adequately addressed, but we took a bold step in the right direction when we committed to this effort. Mass incarceration, excessive penal punishment, disproportionate sentencing (especially death sentences), and police abuse of people of color demonstrate the scope of the problems that continue in American society as a part of the legacy of racial terror to this very day. There is no denying this truth, and we vowed that no energy would be spent trying to do that as we moved forward with these pilgrimages across Georgia.

The pilgrimages began in Macon, Georgia, at the Douglass Theatre, and over the course of the three years they took pilgrims throughout Georgia to many sites where short memorial services were held and historical markers were placed. This way of acknowledging the many lives that were taken because someone had to be sacrificed in order to maintain the status quo of racial apartheid in America served both as a way for all who participated in the pilgrimages to remember and as a way for us to move forward in the work of dismantling the structures that were imagined and constructed during this era to keep African Americans and any other racial minorities designated as undesirable in their place. That place was a place of subjugation and degradation, a place maintained by the terror that was created when folks were forcibly taken from their homes or activities to be killed at the hands of angry mobs. Those mobs were often led by law enforcement or other influential figures in the towns where these crimes were being committed.

These martyrs cannot have died in vain. We were compelled to call their names in services of remembrance and to mark the sites of their sacrifice. Engaging in this effort helped us to reiterate our commitment to the work of dismantling all of the structures that make it possible to denigrate and oppress anyone, especially people of color.

All of the work that is done in reclaiming memory helps to lead the way to hope and racial healing. This work of remembering the lynched supports the effort to disrupt negative energy and create a new narrative, one that makes space for memories that will not allow themselves to be buried. All racial healing must be supported by memory.

Part 8

SINCE IT'S A JOURNEY, STAY READY TO TRAVEL

MEDITATION 43

On the Road Again

It was 2008, and we sat down to take a break because we had done a lot about race. Barack Obama had just been elected president, and in many ways we wanted to believe that we had become a post-racial nation. I can still hear the white voices declaring that we were through with race. We had moved on because a black man and his family were moving into the White House. After all, a descendent of the slave class had done what none of them were ever supposed to do: he had gotten himself elected to the highest office in the land and was moving into a sacred space that had never been meant to be available to members of the group that had been forced to help build the place. Surely race must be settled forever, the thinking went, for one of those descendants had managed to break through the structures designed to keep people of color subjugated. His election was so amazing that it must have been an indication that those structures were gone forever.

If only that analysis had been a description of reality in America, what an even more glorious day Barack Obama's election would have been for the country. But it was not true then, and it is still not true. We are nowhere near being a post-racial country, and we are not even interested in becoming one. However, for many blacks and whites who were ready to see such a change, it was one of the best days of our lives. We will always hold that day close to our hearts as we continue to work for a time when race really will not be the most important thing that we concern ourselves with on a daily basis. On that day we rejoiced. We celebrated. We had hope. We took up Obama's mantra: "Yes we can."

But even as we were celebrating, the voices of resistance had already begun to speak. Some in the congressional leadership declared, even before the ballot boxes were stowed away for the next election, that any legislation President Obama tried to pass was going to be rejected. Just think of that with me for a minute: the election was barely over, yet the lawmaking leadership was declaring that it was not going to cooperate with the newly elected administration. Why? Of course, you could naively argue that it was because they disagreed with his platform. But we know better: they held disdain for him and his black skin. The subtext of their declaration was, *You, black man, managed to seduce the voters, but we are the gatekeepers of racism's legacy, and we will stop you.* Can you hear the message? Their proclamation was accompanied by other denigrating voices around the country before the inauguration: comments about watermelons being planted on the White House lawn, nooses with his photograph attached, doctored photos of the newly elected president looking like their worst idea of someone living in Africa, a man with a bone in his nose and very little clothing. One elected official referred to the First Lady's relatives escaping from the zoo. These unfortunate comments were heartbreaking, outrageous, yet expected by those of us who live with our hearts and minds grounded in an understanding of who we are as a nation. But we kept holding on to the fact that millions of us, black, white, and brown, had voted for this man, and that was not going to be changed by the naysayers.

We can't deny that many who voted for him were unconscious enough to ignore the realities that he would have to navigate. They believed that the light that had come that November morning was going to shine into every crack in the racist constructions of our society and banish the darkness forever. They were mistaken. The darkness was stunned for a moment, but it recovered quickly.

Others of us committed to pray extraordinarily hard that God would keep him, his family, and those around them safe, because we knew his life was in extreme danger. We lived with that angst for eight years, breathed a great sigh of relief when he and his lovely family vacated the premises on that final day, and hoped that the angels, the ancestors, and all of the forces of light—along with the Secret Service—would continue to take care of him and his family.

But as we quickly learned, the darkness had not gone away in those eight years. We had managed to make ourselves believe that it was lessening, but it was not. The election of President Donald J. Trump was darkness's answer to the light, and it was clear that we were being called to get back on the road again. It should not have jolted us as badly as it did, because that is the way the cycle appears to work—the birth-death-rebirth cycle of life in the universe. Some wonderful energy is born, then there is death, and then a chance for rebirth. It is demonstrated in our personal life cycles, and when we pay close attention we recognize it everywhere.

On this journey we arrive somewhere and can sit awhile in the place we have found, and perhaps we can even enjoy a few restful moments. But if we fail to pay attention to the fact that there is still darkness, we will have allowed ourselves to lapse into a space that will not support us. Perhaps racism's relentlessness helps to force all who wish to be conscious to realize that every time we arrive at a resting place, we must stay ready to go back on the road again.

MEDITATION 44

George Floyd Died, So You Need to Stand Still

On May 25, 2020, the world watched a murder. It was not a killing of a kind that we had seen ever before. It was a group of men who had been charged to protect and serve, police officers, who killed a citizen in cold blood while he begged them to help him. He said as many times as he could, "I can't breathe." They paid no attention, especially the senior officer who continued to keep his knee on the man's neck. I can barely stand to write about this today, but it must be reflected upon today and in the years to come. We cannot afford to forget that day's confrontation between the light and darkness. So many of the issues that this entire book has been engaging came to a point on that day. And the world was watching.

On that day, my email and voicemail were inundated with messages of outrage, expressions of grief, and questions. The question most often asked was "What can I do? What can my church, club, community do?" The sense of being desperate and lost prevailed in so many corners. One of the most important gifts that God gave to me during that time was the good sense to be careful about how to answer those "What can I do?" questions. I could not know what those asking the question were able or willing to do in the racial healing arena. There was a lot that I could say to be supportive and to help people begin to ask questions as they explore their ways forward, but I had no prescriptions. Folks were looking for me to have answers that I could not have because the way forward has to evolve for each person. Though one can find help in discerning what to do, each path must be carefully chosen by each of us.

There is a lovely and wise understanding held by some of our Northwest Indigenous siblings about what to do when you are a child lost in the wilderness. They teach that you should stand still, because, you see, the forest is not lost. It knows where you are, and if you will stand still and listen, it will lead you onto the path that gets you back home.

I heard myself repeatedly sharing this story in speeches, in my writings, and in response to people who asked that question in person. Stand still and see what Spirit reveals to you. What do you have the energy to do? Not what knee-jerk response can you make now, when you are in a state of outrage, shock, and horror, but what does your soul need you to do? No one can hear that answer except you.

The question "What can I do?" continues to be very important as we explore all of these issues, which have not changed since George Floyd's death; we have simply, unfortunately, managed to shift them to the edge of consciousness and moved on to the next horrors.

We arrived somewhere on May 25, 2020. But where did we arrive? The answer is multilayered and troublesome, and it will require much more serious reflection to know all or even most of the answer. However, we cannot go away from that day as if nothing happened. Though many forces will challenge us to let it go, to act as if we can go on, and to keep doing whatever else prevents us from thinking too much about it, that will not work. We will continue to have a repeat of state-sanctioned murder, with folks in uniforms killing our young black and brown people under questionable circumstances, as long as we refuse to allow ourselves to reimagine policing and public safety. We can change this narrative whenever we truly decide that we have had enough of it, but we haven't yet; policing is doing exactly what we want it to do. We want to terrorize those who live in black and brown bodies because we as a nation hold the memory of a historical disdain and hatred for those bodies that makes this terrorizing make sense. So we talk about policing and public safety changing without being fully committed to the way such changes will cause us to have to behave differently.

If we can find the courage to say yes to the path that emerges when we stand still and listen, we will depart from the consciousness that accompanied George Floyd's murder and move toward a space that will help us to heal. We can never ignore the invitation to stay ready for departure. In many ways, departing means that we will arrive at a new place that will continue to facilitate our collective healing. If we can learn to live into the deep truth of that process, we can enjoy the journey much more than if we insist on the security of finally arriving at some point and never having to leave again.

As I've said many times in this book, whites often lament that we talk about race too much. Well, blacks and other people of color can conclude that we don't talk about it enough, or that our talking is not leading to the action we need. So we remain in a space that continues to need conversation between people of color and whites. We will be in that space until we dismantle racism and create a world where the love depicted in I Corinthians 13 is a part of the way we live together.

The planet needs all of us to engage in this effort. Can you imagine this world if we are open to a love that transforms us and allows a new kind of light to shine among us?

George Floyd was murdered in cold blood by law enforcement officers who had been charged to protect and serve him, yet who said, in all of our names, "We don't care." What can standing still reveal to us—as individuals, as a nation, as a world—about those officers' attitude toward that commitment, and what does it reveal to us about what is required of us when things like this unfold in front of us? We have many questions to ask of ourselves, and the message to stand still resounds across the land for those whose intention is to listen for the best possible answer.

COVID-19 Invited Us

COVID-19 brought many challenges, but the most profound one for us at the Absalom Jones Center for Racial Healing was the invitation to reinvent ourselves. Here I want to talk about some of the ways that we accepted that invitation, as a way of supporting you if you have made significant changes already or find yourself floundering in the newness of everything that COVID brought about. It is not easy to experience the kind of disruption that was caused by the novel coronavirus as anything but a tragedy. However, we were offered an opportunity to make new choices.

For several months prior to COVID we had been talking a bit about moving some of our work onto a virtual platform. I was not in favor of it at the time, simply because I did not believe that we could offer high-quality classes in dismantling racism and other programs to facilitate transformation without being in the room with the participants. I was wrong! It is not that easy to say "I was wrong" or to change a course of behavior that you thought would never need to change, but COVID made both of those responses necessary, and it continues to do that as we slowly find our pathway back to new ways of being together and working.

COVID-19 delivered its invitation to us in this way: "You are invited to reimagine your work or die." The Center accepted the invitation to reimagine its work. Many blessings have come to the Center because we said yes, even though we went forward with fear and a fair amount of hesitation. Our team of amazing facilitators enthusiastically stepped up to the challenge of making the changes needed to move the dismantling-racism classes onto a virtual platform. Of course, we all wondered how it would work out, but we decided to believe that God would be faithful to us, as has been true since we began this work. We were correct.

Bringing the classes online has meant that we can offer them to many others across the wider church. We've also had reports that this format seems to create even more brave space for participants' genuine expressions of thoughts and feelings—perhaps because of the sense of comfort participants feel by being in the comfort of their homes and other familiar spaces. And the facilitators have been quite pleased with the results of the online classes.

Along with this we have more than doubled our subscribers to our website, which moved from slightly under 5,000 to over 13,000. Our donations tripled because once our online programming was available to participants across the wider church and beyond, many in this expanding audience chose to share their resources generously with the Center in gratitude for its work. Our audience began to include folks from Canada, Latin America, West Africa, Europe, and the Caribbean.

Perhaps my greatest surprise was my ability to learn how to do a few new things on this platform. This was a consequence of the great personal challenge that severe change brings to us. There's no doubt that our comfortable patterns are hard to relinquish. Before COVID, I never scheduled any virtual meetings or made any audio or video recordings. But I received great coaching from a couple of expert young technology coaches. They loved working with me because they said my childlike glee with what I was learning made them happy. I learned to make videos of my short inspirational vignettes and moved on to being able to record sermons and other talks to be sent across the wider church. I was led to navigate my way from skeptic to willing participant in the use of technology as a necessary partner in doing the work of the Center. It is a great tool.

Along with all of this, for which we rejoice, we also grieve. We grieve for the loss of life in our country and across the world from COVID-19, and we grieve for all of the other types of suffering that it brought and continues to bring. We hold the conflicting energy of gratitude and grief in our hands and hearts, and this energy continues to demand that we go deeper into our inner communities and see what we need to address there that will impact our daily lives.

This has been exhibited most profoundly in terms of race. There are many of us who believe that the world's cry of outrage at the murder of George Floyd would not have been the same had we not been in the middle of a pandemic. So many of the defenses that we normally keep in place were gone. Most of us were at home. And everything was turned upside down in our physical and psychological worlds. All this contributed to the manner in which the world became mobilized around his murder. While there is certainly no concrete way to truly assess whether this is true, we know that hundreds of young black and brown people have been killed by police since George Floyd and we barely know their names. There was some dynamic in that moment in May 2020 that made things different.

What was your response to COVID-19? What did it invite you to change? How did it impact your thoughts and concerns around race and the other justice issues that occupy so much of our time and attention? What did you do to answer that invitation or to avoid it? How are you continuing to respond to it? How has your view of the world been impacted by the presence of COVID?

MEDITATION 46

Do You Really Want Reparations or Not?

Over the years, I have participated in many discussions about reparations. Often they begin with a question about how white folks could figure out a painless way to give all of the descendants of slaves some type of monetary compensation for their ancestors' freedom and dignity being taken away from them. The conversations that begin in this way seem much more about trying to find the easiest way to assuage white guilt about benefiting from the establishment of white supremacy rule in this land. Such conversations produce no productive path to follow because they are not focused upon finding viable solutions.

There are many questions to be asked and answered about how to work to repair the breach caused by slavery. The first and most important one is how to calculate what the loss of freedom and dignity is worth in dollars and cents. What amount of money would we receive because our ancestors were stolen from their homeland and subjected to chattel slavery? What will this payment be an attempt to cover? How can anyone be repaid for the loss of their chance to be who God put them on the earth to be? I believe this trend of thinking that money alone will be able to fix the country's equity problems is woefully inadequate. We need whites in the United States to step up and address the deeper issues about how to repair the breach created by the white supremacist attitude that supported slavery and all the oppressive structures that emerged from that way of thinking and which continue to thrive in the twenty-first century.

It is wearying to watch so many efforts to acknowledge the wrongs done to Africans stolen from their land, brought to the United States, and forced to help build it into what it is today. A discussion about a few million dollars being allocated by Congress for compensation to slaves' descendants is insufficient. But no such plan will amount to anything more than a handful of semi-progressive white people being able to feel a little less guilty in the short term while the structures that continue to oppress the descendants of our enslaved ancestors maintain the white supremacy status quo.

A genuine conversation about reparations demands a willingness to consider deep systemic changes in the way that all our systems are structured. White people who think they are ready to engage in this conversation with the hope of actually doing the work required to make changes need to be willing to see the world in a new way. We cannot tidy up the current oppressive system by simply allocating a few dollars to build some structure of tribute to a black person or offering a few scholarships or small payouts to a handful of descendants of enslaved persons. While these efforts can be a sign of good intentions if they are paired with genuine actions to make the needed systemic changes in the country, generally they are merely superficial. For genuine and sustainable reparations to work, white people who have begun to awaken to the world created for them by stolen labor must begin destabilizing all of the systems in the United States that prevent everyone, especially people of African descent, from having equal access to freedom and liberation.

This country needs a new way to be; the COVID-19 pandemic has made that crystal clear to anyone who did not see it before. The pandemic presented us with stark confirmation of the health, education, and economic inequalities in this country; the most astounding one is the discrepancy in the death rates between whites, blacks, and other people of color. It has become quite clear to many of us that one of the reasons there was such a cavalier attitude in so many places about resuming business as usual so early in the pandemic, despite the additional tens of thousands of deaths that it would cause, was that a large percentage of those who were most at risk were people of color and the elderly, groups that are seen as expendable.

Thus, progressive whites who wish for a society that is honest about doing reparations must be willing to understand that such a society will have no persons who are deemed expendable. What do we have to do in the United States to change our understanding of having expendable people? This is a question to be deeply pondered by all of us and especially progressive white people in our faith communities because eliminating a sense of hierarchy in the value of the population is a true first and important step in repairing the wide breach between us.

These days, I find that I am most interested in speaking to people who profess to have faith and an interest in practicing that faith with integrity. I believe that the honest work of reparations begins with a willingness to take the bold step of accepting that the present way of life that we have created in the United States is not going to support honest reparations work. The work requires one to find the courage to ask very hard questions about all facets of our system while moving into the place of being willing to see them changed.

The conversation on reparations will not be genuine until it begins with concern for people of African descent about the ways the United States is going to assure affordable health care, equitable education, affordable housing, living wages, access to transportation, and safe neighborhoods that are free from state-supported violence against our black bodies. And African Americans must have all of the other necessities needed to live fully into God's intention for them. Until such time that we begin this conversation with the intent to build a new world where justice and love prevail, we are playing a strange and tiring game. Hopefully, folks who have faith are not really interested in living a lie and would like to do this work for real. It remains to be seen.

If the work toward reparations is not grounded in a new way of seeing, with new light shining in the hearts of white people and making the quest for justice sustainable, the efforts to repair will remain superficial. But if whites, both individually and collectively, take this path seriously, it will release much new energy that can be used to reimagine this journey for all, and that will gladden the heart of God. So let's talk about reparations.

Sick and Tired of Being Sick and Tired

Our warrior woman mother Fannie Lou Hamer made the words "sick and tired of being sick and tired" famous years ago when she declared them in regard to the long, protracted struggle that she endured during her life. Many will recall her at the Democratic National Convention in the early 1960s helping to wage the battle for blacks from Mississippi to have a right to be recognized there, as they deserved to be. In addition to engaging in that type of public witnessing, she suffered great personal loss when she was beaten almost to death and expelled from her sharecropper's dwelling because she chose to register to vote. She suffered a stroke as a result of the beating and lived the remainder of her life having to navigate the effects of that abuse.

Black people and other people of color who are paying attention can declare, "I am sick and tired of being sick and tired." It is difficult to live in a black or brown body in a land that has deemed folks with that kind of skin as "other." Earlier I noted my oldest son's lament on the day after the Mother Emanuel Church massacre in Charleston in 2015: "Mama, it is so hard to be black in America." While there is an endless list of particulars behind both of these assessments, the main and most profound issue is a matter that cannot be remedied, and that is having black skin.

So when a white person says with a sense of soul weariness, "I am tired of talking about race," and chooses to set aside the discussion for a season, it is an interesting issue for blacks who are trying to be in solidarity with whites to process. We would wish for each person to do whatever is necessary to make sure their soul is nourished, but on the other hand, part of being a fellow pilgrim involves engaging the pain of the journey. Personally, while I want my white fellow pilgrims to be sure to take care of themselves, I also want them to acknowledge what a grand whites-only privilege it is to be able to leave the entire racial arena and return to it as they choose to do so. That is a privilege that I and every other black person do not have because we carry our skin with us wherever we go. So while I would encourage the white person to take the break, I would ask them to allow it to be informed by this fact.

One way I can relate to how this might be for them is my consciousness about my friends who live without shelter. I love the rain. For me, there is nothing better than a rainy day: a good book, a lit candle, maybe even a fire if it is chilly enough, a pot of something cooking to make the house smell good. But for my friends living without shelter, is a horrible and very uncomfortable day. I hold sadness in my heart about that for them. I cannot stop the rain, and for the most part I cannot provide shelter for them, but I can hold them in my heart as I embrace the day I described. Yes, it changes the day for me, as it should. The main point of awakening is that you see things differently. So I hold the day in a new way. I still find it a lovely day, the soup pot still smells wonderful, and my candles still burn throughout the day. But my friends are named as a part of my day in a way that was not possible before I met them. My sense of gratitude, of not taking any part of the gift of the day for granted, is deepened. I am enriched by holding both my love of the rain and the care for my friends in tension in my heart. I believe that this gladdens the Creator's heart as well, but whether it does or not, it is the right thing to do. It is what consciousness brought by the light that comes in the morning demands.

So I think of this when whites try to explain how difficult it is to really know what it's like to be a black person in America. Actually, it is not that hard. After all, we are not a different species; we are just humans, like everyone else. That is the first thing to clearly acknowledge. Then it is important to move on to understanding that emotions and the soul work required of all of us have no ethnic origin and are not bound in any way to fit into the artificial categories that we have created to define, control, manage, and in many cases subjugate others. All of the human valuation metrics that exist in a racially stratified culture are indefensible and need to be deconstructed and reimagined. This is simply the bottom line, and each individual can take personal responsibility to work on this regardless of what the collective response might be.

As I stated in the very first meditation, the place to begin is with the journey into your own inner community, because the truths that you find there can be globalized. When you discover what makes you peaceful, you can imagine that to be true for others regardless of their race. Things such as peace, contentment, patience, love, hope, fear, courage, gratitude, and so much more have nothing to do with skin color—or culture, for that matter. These are personal responses, and each person needs to take responsibility for themselves regarding them. It is not as difficult as it has been made to sound. For instance, the proclamation "I can't ever know what it is like to be black" appears to be more of a confession of a sense of inadequacy than anything else. Let's take a deeper look at this, because it is crucial to healing.

If you are white and have a child, think about your connection to that child. You are committed to making sure that their life progresses in the best possible ways. When you think of other people who are white and who have children, do you have difficulty imagining how they might feel about them? Do you imagine that they care about the children and wish the best for them just as you do? Now, can you ask yourself why there should be any difference in the way a black or brown person would feel about their children? If something in you believes that there is a difference, then it might be a good exercise to explore what you imagine those differences to be and why you believe them to exist. You could engage in this exercise with grief, loneliness, hope, fear, rage, anxiety, joy, or peace: the list is endless.

This is the work of putting your feet into the shoes of those designated as "other" and walking a few miles in them until you have a real sense of all of the threads that might link you to them. This exercise can be helpful no matter who is being considered, because until we allow ourselves to delve deeply into other people's journey in our imagination, we don't have any idea who they are or how they might experience the journey of life. We think we know the folks who look more like us and are in close proximity to us because we focus on the things that we have in common and make projections based upon those perceived outer connecting factors. But for the most part, that is not correct; we are not seeing the person who really exists in that body, even though we may share skin color, gender, socioeconomic status, education, and so on.

We are simply relating to the imagined person we have created in our own heads. Instead, we should take the time to do the slow work of allowing the real person to reveal to us who they really are.

In the same way, blacks and other people of color are challenged to be careful not to simply relate to whites in terms of who they are imagined to be. Many blacks, especially but not only younger persons, have come to a place of being quite clear about their fatigue with white people's unconsciousness. Many of them clearly state that they no longer have much energy or interest in trying to help whites manage their journey with race. I understand; this has been a fifty-year journey for me, so I get the fatigue. But I am aware that we stand on the shoulders of a great cloud of witnesses who left us a legacy of resistance and survival that deserves careful caretaking. It deserves to have us build on it in whatever ways we are called to do so.

Protecting this legacy is important to me, and being well and empowered are important parts of the equation for me. I am quite clear that choosing to have empathy for another human, no matter their race or stage in life, is a part of the process necessary for me to be well; that is a choice I can make. No one, regardless of skin color, class, gender, physical ability, or age, is exempted from the work of helping to create a sustainable world. Such a world will not be possible as long as there are large groups of people who are deemed less valuable than other groups and expendable. That position has led us to this day of polarization, hatred, paranoia, war, addictions, and so many other ways to destroy ourselves. While black people are not responsible for white folks in any way, we are all responsible for ourselves. We seem to rush past that reality a bit too rapidly at times. Black people and other people of color do not get to avoid the work because of the oppression suffered by the group.

Rather than simply concluding that we have had enough and are off to another agenda, it seems that the better response is to stand still and inquire of the Creator and the Ancestors about what they might want to see us do. We have our work to do, and it is about all of us. It is not only up to whites, as it may have been made to seem in the past. We need to reimagine the work, and that requires asking a new set of questions, telling our truths in a new way, listening more carefully to the call from the Spirit, and working to create new narratives. We cannot simply decide to take a seat at tables that did not deserve to exist in the first place because they were not actually about life in the way that would benefit all of us. If we all do our work, then we will have a more equitable basis for creating a new foundation that can support us and help to make our world a more sustainable place for everyone.

It is very important for everyone, black, white, or brown, to remember that empathy is a choice. Being well is better than not being well, and being an empowered person on this planet is available to everyone. It can be accessed by any and all persons who choose to embark upon that path. It requires intention, vigilance, and responsibility, and it will take a lifetime. As we walk that path, we will arrive at the doors of places we hope could be our final destination, only to find that we are led to explore more of the journey. But we can be assured that the journey will be well traveled if we embrace it as best we can in all the ways revealed to us by asking honest questions and allowing our hearts to stay open to hear the answers.

MEDITATION 48

Our Island Home Needs Us

There is a lovely line in Rite II of the Episcopal Liturgy that says, "At your command all things came to be: the vast expanse of interstellar space, galaxies, suns, the planets in their courses, and this fragile earth, our island home. By your will they were created and have their being."[24] There surely might be other worlds to explore, other worlds where we might live, but I am not especially concerned with that at this point. The major point to be made is that we are here, and we are challenged to make this space sustainable. It is clear that we have done a poor job of taking care of our island home over the course of time.

It seems important to me that we not allow ourselves to be seduced by a handful of rich white men who are preoccupied with finding a way to relocate themselves and their friends to other galaxies in an effort to avoid the work here that needs to be done. It is the human response to make a mess of something and then start the process of trying to find an alternative, rather than being willing to sit with the task of finding a remedy for the problem that we created. The answer to our earth-keeping problems cannot be relocation. Instead, we need to learn from our mistakes, and we need to listen for remedies that come from the heart and core of our very being.

So, we have journeyed together to this final meditation. Thank you. Readers will have read these words in many different ways.

You could have read the book in its entirety in one sitting, or over the course of a few days or weeks. Perhaps you read it with others in a book study group, or periodically as a devotional reader. Or it could be that it was a resource for you that you picked up here and there when you were so moved. I am grateful for you and your attention regardless of the way that you engaged it, and I am grateful for your willingness to embrace the issues raised in these pages, which have so much to do with the continued survival of this planet and the quality of our lives on it. My gratitude is extended to you for your willingness to be on a journey and for whatever commitments you have made to search for the light in as many places as possible. Hopefully, unlike Mulla Nasrudin, who lost his keys indoors but looked for them outdoors because the light was better there, you are committed to looking in the right places for the key to your heart's deepest longing: to help create a sustainable world. Dr. Martin Luther King Jr. told us a long time ago that we can work to create a community, or we can work to create and sustain chaos. My work leads me to believe that we can decide where our focus will be, and that this decision will be deeply rooted in the state of our inner community as we navigate our journey of life.

The greatest sustainability is possible when the people are strong, are willing to name the energies that are not interested in being in the light, and call them out in the public sphere so that everyone can see their negativity for what it is. When folks are feeling disconnected from their inner community, they find it difficult to welcome the light when it shows up, because it causes too much conflict for them. So it is crucial to find light-filled examples in the external world to confirm to ourselves that engaging light-filled lives is possible.

Imagine how tired the bubbly, cheery person makes you feel on Monday morning when you would rather be anywhere else. In the same way, when you are feeling separated from your inner community, it is not a good time to imagine a highly functioning outer community. The way that inner reality and outer reality intersect has been one of the major threads throughout all of these meditations because it is critical, because it does not get talked about enough, and because it is often misunderstood. This lack of understanding leads people to conclude that there is only the outer world to embrace, and when that happens much conflict can arise.

Racism and all of its relatives need to be banished from the planet, but it is not going anyplace except insofar as individuals stand up to it and declare their willingness to be on a healing journey. The rhythms of arrivals and departures on this journey make it possible for new energy to be generated, and that supports courage and intention. This will allow the challenges to the status quo that will help to set us free.

We can barely imagine the new world that has to come into being, because we have never seen it before. We think that the power dynamics that have been at play for so long in our world must be the only way. But this can only be true if we allow creativity and imagination to be killed by the negative energy that manifests as long nights of intractable darkness. Our imaginations will argue with us that more is possible, and we will need to listen to those arguments if we want a different world.

No one can be forced into wellness. Remember that lovely story mentioned earlier about Jesus and the lame brother at the Pool of Bethesda. It is so instructive for all of us. Jesus said to him,

"Do you want to be healed?" With that question comes a shift of energy, from lament (which is fine at times, but not this time) to the possibility of creating a different narrative. We can ask similar questions: Do you want to be healed, America? Do you want to become a post-racial society? Former slave states, do you want to be rid of the legacy of slavery? Episcopal Church, do you want to facilitate healing for the damage done in the schools that denigrated and injured Native children? Seminaries, do you want to train a group of leaders who will ask hard new questions that have more to do with the twenty-first century than with centuries that have already come and gone? Organized religion, do you want to know what new thing God has in mind for you in the twenty-first century? Those of you who have barricaded yourselves in homogeneous enclaves of fear, do you want to be well? Black women and men, do you want to find the balm that will heal the wounds left by slavery that make it easier to denigrate one another than to see each other as God's beloved children? Whites who believe that your white skin is best, do you want to be healed? Native people who have been devastated by the theft of your land, do you wish to be well? Asian and Latinx folks who have had your voices of healing taken, do you want to be well?

If the answers to these questions are yes, then the most basic next question is what we must do to get into the healing pool. How can we say yes to the angel's invitation to avail ourselves of the pool's healing waters? What do we need to help us move ourselves into that pool? Can we find the help we need?

The answer, according to Dr. Howard Thurman, one of our most important mentors, is that God always answers the person who is praying. So if you are asking these questions with the prayerful intention of finding an answer—if you really do wish to get into the pool of healing waters because you are genuinely sick and tired of being sick and tired—then you will be answered.

When it comes to racism's hold on us, what does it mean to wish to be well in the twenty-first century? A part of what it means is that all ideas that support superiority and inferiority have to be banished. If being well becomes a core principle, there will be no place for a hierarchical way of evaluating one another. The Creator has made everyone, and all of the folks on the planet are beloved. There is no energy being sent from the Creator to support seeing some people as more valuable than others, because everyone is equally valuable and no one is expendable. This challenging idea leads to the next logical place, which is for us to learn how to want the best for everyone on the earth. It means being willing to make a commitment to equity. It means that we are glad to see others gain access to whatever they need to thrive in their lives.

Getting well means breaking the bonds of captivity generated by systems that oppress and wound all of us. It means that we will affirm that we are on a journey that embraces the long nights of brokenness and holds on to the notion that light will come in the morning. Even though we are not sure exactly which morning will bring the light, we know that it will come. We will be able to declare with amazing certainty that each step that we take on the healing path will help to disrupt the darkness. We will know that being relentless in our efforts to stand in solidarity with one another is in fact a part of what has to be done in order to make sure that this earth, our island home, can continue.

Getting well means affirming that we cannot live as the Creator intended without being willing to care about one another. It means affirming that everyone's healing and possibilities for being well are inextricably linked together, whether or not we like it or acknowledge it. We know that imagination and faith can make a difference, and that light is coming in the morning.

AFTERWORD

Now that you have come to the end of these meditations, I hope that you have been disturbed, comforted, and led to a new level of intention and inspiration. I hope that the encounter with the stories, ideas, and analysis in these pages will be something that you can call upon as you pick up the fire extinguisher and help quell the house fire.

Neither our country nor our planet can sustain the negative energy that we generate by assuming that fostering hatred, discord of every type, and even murder is a remedy for living together. We are here together, and that fact will never change. Hatred and fear are far greater enemies to sustainability than any one group of human beings is to another group.

These meditations are the best effort that I know how to make at telling the truth, because I trust that the truth will set us free. We decide how much of the truth to allow into our hearts, and that depends mostly on our willingness to be disrupted. Disruption in our personal way of being leads us to change, and that will lead to change in the outer world because our new way of seeing will demand it.

Activism is critical, but it has to be grounded in inner change in order to be sustained. Our history bears witness to this truth: consider how much our country has changed for the better in some periods but gone backward in others. Inner life and outer expressions of life always mirror each other, as our commitment to violence and discord today demonstrates. Our country's mental health issues bear witness to the fact that we have much inner discord to embrace and seek to heal.

I hope that you are one of the people who enthusiastically say, "I want to be well!" And I hope that you are willing to do whatever inner work that it takes to respond to the cultural house fire, as well as moving from that inner work to outer activism. My most sincere hopes and prayers are that this book has opened up a door, a window, or even just a tiny space where light can shine that was not present before you read it, and that this light will become stronger and stronger as you go forward.

May you be a half shade braver each day as you pick up the fire extinguisher.

NOTES

1. Edward C. Whitmont, *The Symbolic Quest* (Princeton, NJ: Princeton University Press, 1969), 160.
2. Whitmont, *The Symbolic Quest*, 156.
3. Erica Cirino, "Why Am I So Angry?," *Healthline*, last updated March 29, 2019, https://www.healthline.com/health/why-am-i-so-angry.
4. William Grier and Price Cobbs, *Black Rage* (New York: Basic Books, 1968).
5. Martin Luther King Jr., *Letter from Birmingham Jail* (Stamford, CT: Overbrook Press, 1968).
6. Clark E. Moustakas, *Loneliness and Love* (Englewood Cliffs, NJ: Prentice-Hall, 1972), 20–21.
7. Parker Palmer, *The Promise of Paradox: A Celebration of the Contradictions in the Christian Life* (South Bend, IN: Ave Maria Press, 1980).
8. Rainer Maria Rilke, *Letter to a Young Poet* (New York: Norton, 1954).
9. *Without Sanctuary: Lynching Photography in America* (Santa Fe, NM: Twin Palms, 2000).
10. Lillian Smith, *The Killers of the Dream* (New York: W. W. Norton, 1994).
11. Sheila Rowe, *Healing Racial Trauma: The Road to Resilience* (Downers Grove, IL: Inter-Varsity Press, 2020), 10.
12. Rowe, *Healing Racial Trauma*, 12.
13. Christina Feldman and Jack Kornfield, *Stories of the Spirit, Stories of the Heart: Parables of the Spiritual Path from Around the World* (San Francisco: Harper, 1991), 99.
14. Brother Lawrence, *The Practice of the Presence of God*, translated by Robert Edmondson (Orleans, MA: Paraclete, 2007).
15. David Whyte, *River Flow* (Langley, WA: Many Rivers Press, 2007), 362.
16. Martin Luther King Jr., *Where Do We Go from Here: Chaos or Community?* (New York: Harper & Row, 1967).
17. Howard Thurman, *Jesus and the Disinherited* (Boston: Beacon Press, 1976).
18. Marco Williams, dir., *Banished*, PBS, 2008, https://www.pbs.org/independent lens/documentaries/banished/.
19. Zora Neale Hurston, *Their Eyes Were Watching God* (New York: Lippincott, 1937).
20. Martin Doblmeier, dir., *Backs Against the Wall: The Howard Thurman Story*, Journey Films, 2019, https://www.imdb.com/title/tt9376890/.
21. Derrick A. Bell, "Who's Afraid of Critical Race Theory?," *University of Illinois Law Review*, 1995, 893–910.
22. Kathy Russell-Cole, Midge Wilson, and Ronald E. Hall, *The Color Complex* (New York: Anchor Books, 2013).

23. "Big Bill Broonzy: Black, Brown, and White," YouTube, posted by HaloedG, January 23, 2009, https://www.youtube.com/watch?v=k0cIc0ZsTLA.

24. *The Episcopal Book of Common Prayer* (New York: Church Publishing, 2016), 370.